The New Classics

The New Classics

FRESH IDEAS FOR ROOMS THAT ENDURE

SUZANNE TROCMÉ

Photography by
KEN HAYDEN

Stewart, Tabori & Chang
New York

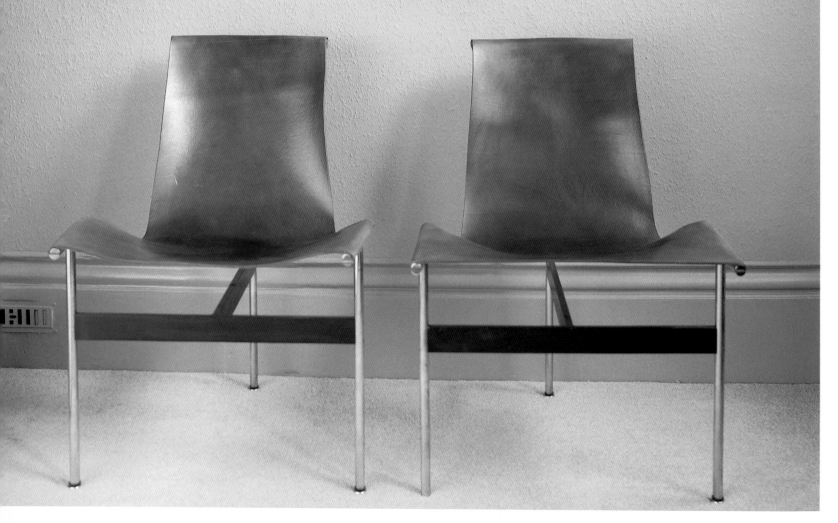

Produced by Jacqui Small
Project Editor Catherine Rubinstein
Editor Jude Garlick
Designer Robin Rout
Production Geoff Barlow

Published in 2002 by
Stewart, Tabori & Chang
A Company of La Martinière Groupe
115 West 18th Street
New York, NY 10011

Canadian Distribution:
Canadian Manda Group
One Atlantic Avenue, Suite 105
Toronto, Ontario M6K 3E7
Canada

Library of Congress Cataloging-in-Publication Data
Trocmé, Suzanne.
  New classics : fresh ideas for rooms that endure /
  by Suzanne Trocmé ; photographs by Ken Hayden.
    p. cm.
  Includes index.
  ISBN 1-58479-155-1
    1. Interior decoration—History—20th century. I
. Hayden, Ken. II. Title.

NK1980 .T765 2002
747—dc21   2002066959

The text of this book was composed in Joanna.

Printed in China

10 9 8 7 6 5 4 3 2 1

First Printing

**To my darling Paul, and
the boys, Miles and Edwin**

CONTENTS

WHAT IS A NEW CLASSIC?

What is it about the "little black dress" that makes it a classic? Is it the blackness of the dress, or its simplicity, or the fact that it can be adapted for different occasions? Probably all of these. The blackness flatters the figure; an interior, by contrast, benefits from space-enhancing whites and paler neutrals. In other respects a classic home is like the dress, and should be unfussy and adaptable for different occasions and functions.

Little black dresses are not all the same, and the effect of a dress depends upon the spirit in which it is worn. There is an old adage that if a woman walks into a room and is complimented on her dress, then it is not a good dress; if she is told that *she* looks good, the dress is a success. A little black dress has the power to make the wearer's personality shine through, if chosen well, and is always stylish, provided it fits properly and the form is appropriate to the wearer. In all instances, the dress is designed for the woman, not the other way around. For a home interior to endure, it too has to suit its wearer, the inhabitant.

In any context, a classic is something of established excellence, a standard work against which others are measured, or something quintessentially definitive or typical—of the highest class or rank. Within the realm of architecture and interior design, it is something of soul and integrity that endures. Without the test of

time, it can be hard to recognize a classic while it is young—classic is not the same as popular—but any new classic that is recognizable is worth preserving. A classic, be it a building, a work of art or a chair, deserves scrutiny for its meaning (including its historical import), its beauty, its function, and its harmony of proportion; a new classic must have all of these, but also be adapted to modern times.

Classics tend to preserve themselves, but they sometimes need a helping hand in the form of restoration or even reinvention, alteration in materials or scale to suit modern life and respond to technological advances. Domestic architecture retains its basic requirements: a place to sleep, prepare food, eat, and sometimes work; a place that has light and is protected from the weather and other natural inconveniences. But the social aspect of the interior is forever changing in response to the way we live. Perhaps the beauty and harmony of our environments lies in the architecture, or the chair itself; perhaps other ornamentation is not a prerequisite for living. There is luxury in discipline. A new classic life is as much a state of mind as a choice of environment.

There is a difference, of course, between "classic" and "classical," yet it seems to me that many new classics have their roots in classical Greece. Some of the most admired modern-looking designs were inspired by ancient lifestyles.

Although we know, for example, that India brought the West exquisite silks and cottons, we forget how it also inspired Art Deco architects, or how Africa inspired the Cubists. The Egyptians built post-and-lintel temples that could be mistaken for twentieth-century buildings. Greek artistry, coupled with Roman building techniques, continues to be not only a source of inspiration but also a blueprint for architecture and design.

Furthermore, the ancient Greeks understood well-being. Their curved *klismos* chair, for example, supported the back well. But to the Greeks, the visual effect and resultant mental harmony were just as important as ergonomics. The rhythm of line of their architecture and furniture is a pattern for visual harmony, symmetry supporting the balance of mind and body.

This balance and harmony of proportion is known in the world of architecture as eurythmy. The term also refers to a system of rhythmical body movements performed to a recitation of verse or prose. A classic interior needs its own rhythm, and our movement in it needs syncopation: rooms we enjoy for activity have a different beat from those for repose. In accentual verse, a rhythm is the pattern created by the arrangement of stressed and unstressed syllables; in quantative verse it is the pattern of long and short syllables. The former description could represent one kind of classic interior, where furniture and form grow from feeling, and the latter another, where disciplines of order and restraint create a pattern for living.

Eurythmy became topical again in the early twentieth century, when Austrian philosopher and educator Rudolf Steiner suggested physical movements that follow patterns of spoken speech and musical tones to promote health. Today much is achieved in education for the intellect, but general well-being is neglected. One starting point has to be the home: instead of promoting "lifestyle," we need to educate people to feel life through art and environment, through interiors that express their harmony by their fluidity of design. Physical form is built out of movement that has come to rest. It is eurythmy that we aim for in the new classic home.

In scrutinizing new classic interiors, I have also observed the people who create and commission them. It takes talent to form a multifaceted home into a fluid whole. A mere collection of beautiful furniture is not enough, nor does it make for well-being. But there is no blueprint: these interiors cannot be pigeonholed, and can be emulated only to a limited extent, since they rely not only upon each element within, and the space and architecture around, but also upon the manner and spirit in which they were created. A home is for good living—choose it well, wear it well, and it will be a good interior.

BELOW A delightful pair of chairs by American furniture designer Paul McCobb exhibit good proportion and line, combining beauty with honesty of function and form. His low-priced furniture brought Modernist design to the public in the 1950s. The "Planner Group" (1950), in traditional birch and maple, uses simple construction in an undecorated, modular fashion.

Pairs of mirrors, urns, and eighteenth-century Swedish chairs symmetrically flank the fireplace in a living room created for much-traveled fashion designers, who use it mainly for entertaining. Adhering to classical principles, comfortable contemporary linen slipcovered seating is also symmetrical in this square room with its original ceiling. Neoclassical images and sculpture add to the drama of an elegant and comfortable setting.

INTERIORS

A classic interior can take many guises, depending on personal taste and the way we choose to live. All rooms should be comfortable, and for some people, physical comfort is the predominant aim of their chosen scheme; for others, control or order guides the presentation of an interior, producing a different type of psychological comfort; and for others still, it takes drama or the ultimate in elegance to fulfill their needs.

"For there is a music wherever there is a harmony, order or proportion; and thus far we may maintain the music of the spheres; for those well-ordered motions, and regular paces, though they give no sound unto the ear, yet to the understanding they strike a note most full of harmony."

SIR THOMAS BROWNE, SEVENTEENTH-CENTURY ENGLISH AUTHOR AND PHYSICIAN

ORDER

Man has sought order since our first attempts to rationalize our presence on Earth. Throughout history and in the modern world, we have tried to escape the disorder and confusion of chaos, in practical as much as in philosophical terms. A new, empty living space whose lack of shape cries out for an architect's order is as much a form of chaos as is a cluttered home whose design and functionality have gone stale.

The need for order lies deep within us, in our homes as in every other aspect of life from time immemorial. Against a backdrop of the regularity of most heavenly bodies, the ancients witnessed the passing of clouds, rain, lightning, shooting stars, the occasional comet and, horror of horrors, the fearful phenomenon of a solar eclipse. Faced with this confusing multiplicity, beyond their physical power to control, they sought to master it, symbolically at least, by imposing order. They constructed a cosmology (the Greek word *kosmos* means both order and universe), relating the parts to each other and to themselves and welding them into a conceptual whole.

Hesiod, the father of Greek didactic poetry (and my favorite dead mentor) flourished around the eighth century B.C. In his *Theogeny*, he describes the origin of the universe out of Chaos, the infinite empty space that existed before all things. Chaos was not, according to Hesiod, a void: rather like a new home or empty living space, it had form and character—and it was filled with clouds and darkness. Hundreds of years later, the Roman poet Ovid (43 B.C.–A.D. 17) described Chaos as the original shapeless mass into which the architect of the world introduced order and harmony, and from which individual forms were made.

Cosmos, in contrast to Chaos, came to represent the orderly universe and cosmology: the framework of concepts and relationships that we erect, satisfying emotional or intellectual need, to bring descriptive order into our world and establish our place in it. Cosmologies invented by man throughout history inevitably reflect the physical and intellectual environment of the time, including society's interests and culture. In relation to both immediate surroundings and the wider context, we draw upon the same thought processes.

When designing an interior, we are responding to and projecting our personal, often subconscious, "cosmology": our deep-seated need for order—not necessarily in terms of being strictly organized, but at least in terms of arranging things so that they make sense to us and show some coherence—and our sense of priorities and values. Unspoken philosophies reveal themselves in myriad subtle ways in the contemporary classic interior; rationality is every bit as fundamental as beauty.

BELOW Even a room with an ethnic flavor and incorporating rustic elements—with straw cushions for summer months and an African stool—can be an ordered one if attention is paid to the proportions of its elements and the space between the objects, so maintaining a general sense of uniformity. Eight black-and-white etchings by Ian McKeever are positioned in two strictly symmetrical groups of four on each side of the mirror.

A STRICT REGIME

The "cosmology" of the apartment created by Robert Bray and Mitchell Turnbough, of New York-based architects Bray-Schaible, shows a strict sense of order, inspired by the fastidiousness of its inhabitant, a fashion executive whose career demands that he be stylish and decisive. "We took our cue from his relentless organization," says Bray. This is a person who reads a book, then discards it; lives for the present; and has little mind for accident or adventure: he wanted something minimal but not stark.

The apartment, in a "spectacularly mediocre" 1948 building on New York's East Side, is small—two rooms plus kitchen, bathroom, and dressing room. Everything has its place: there can be little flexibility, since the occupant's activities are habitual and the space diminutive.

Bray knows that the expression of good architecture in a small space is just as important as in a grander one: "If you have a few large-scale things, a room looks bigger." In one room, three two-seater settees surround a large, square ottoman; a long table doubles as a desk along

the fourth side. In line with the table, a cantilevered console runs along the wall. All furniture is below waist height, so nothing impedes the line of sight except a Richard Giglio painting, the sole focal point. A midnight-black carpet extends from wall to wall, creating drama and contrast.

In the bedroom is a bed with a chocolate leather base and headboard, chairs, a television, and two tables displaying antique and colored vintage glass—a humanizing element and the only references to the past. The walk-in

The impact of this living room derives from the confident, orderly positioning of three identical two-seater sofas around a leather ottoman, their uniform height creating a strong horizon line. The shade lowers to allow daylight in, but blocks the view so the focus remains inward.

closet is a paean to systematic storage, its contents concealed behind slinky brown velvet curtains that glide at a touch.

Despite this strict regime, the apartment is warm and inviting, easy on the eye and designed for living. The sofas are comfortable; there is a variety of textures— cotton velvet, wool, and leather— and the color scheme is neutral. It is both glamorous and functional. If it were a garment, it would be a highly tailored gentleman's suit, independent of fashion or accessory and cut close to the skin.

ABOVE There is no room for overflow in this apartment, and no clutter; newspapers, for instance, are discarded immediately after reading. This presented quite a challenge for the distinguished architectural firm of Bray-Schaible, since everything had to find a permanent place—and the project happened to be the smallest the firm had ever taken on. Undeterred, they intentionally chose furniture of a grand scale, to make the space seem more generous. In the bedroom, the headboard height matches that of the chairs; the bedside tables were custom-made to meet the room's requirements. The red glass provides accent color.

ABOVE The essentially two-roomed apartment has a dressing room-closet off the bedroom. Acres of jackets hang directly above their coordinating pants "organized by fabric, color, and weight," circumnavigating the room in swathes of color and complementary textures. The whole array is completely hidden by dense chocolate-brown velvet draperies.

LEFT In this duplex, furniture is intended to be flexible: a high-backed sofa on castors by Philippe Starck and a low-backed equivalent can shift easily, even spin around, to accommodate different guest arrangements. A pair of Cuban mahogany "Chinese Box" tables by Bonhotal appear like dice that have tumbled into the space, yet a sense of order prevails. Cabinets are avoided in favor of a storage unit under the raised platform.

BELOW Pillows stacked as sculpture can be added to the scene at a moment's notice—they are neat in their accessibility and form. The black leather-upholstered "Milano" sofa from Zanotta has become a design classic; the arm pads, which are in fact cushions, are held in place with Velcro and are simple to remove. Angled lamps, here Artimide's "Tolemeo," are useful in any interior since the light can be thrown in a different direction with ease.

SIMPLICITY AND FLEXIBILITY

Functionality was key for interior designer Jean-Dominique Bonhotal, who took his inspiration from the Shakers when designing his apartment overlooking the pretty Parc Monceau in Paris. "Everything they did was simple and functional, to keep their minds focused on higher things," he explains. His aim was to create order: "I had to step back and observe myself," he says. What he saw was a single man, or *célibataire*, unencumbered by possessions and with a practical turn of mind.

In contrast to much of his work in Europe and Arab countries with antiques of great value and exotic collections and fabrics, Bonhotal thought it appropriate for his own apartment to have a contemporary décor, but not stereotypically or clinically ultramodern. He chose oak as the unifying material. His objective was an apartment that was stark and simple, a calm and neutral space that would not influence his work. The many rooms embrace twenty-first-century mobility: seating areas are defined yet expandable, and furniture can be moved around or removed easily—most pieces are on castors—to accommodate guests.

Bonhotal was fortunate in that little remained of the building's original Second Empire (mid-

A cinnamon carpet warms an ordered grouping of furniture. Instead of hanging traditionally, pictures stand on a ledge at one end of the room beside a low fireplace, modernizing an old apartment. The blue painting, in acrylic on wood, entitled *Enfermée dans un monde et regarder ailleurs* ("Enclosed in a world and looking elsewhere"), is by Christine Legois-Bonhotal, a professor of plastic arts and the designer's sister. The tables with tops of black lacquered steel lattice and bases in light oak are by Bonhotal, as are the sheepskin-covered stools.

nineteenth-century) character; otherwise, he would have felt duty-bound to restore it. Originally a *hôtel particulier* or courtyarded mansion for one family, during the 1930s it was transformed into smaller residential units. Bonhotal now occupies three of these—two adjoining each other on the upper level and a single one beneath them—which he has combined to form a duplex apartment. On the

upper level is the living room, plus bedrooms, bathrooms, and a small kitchen; on the lower level an office, kitchen, and palatial dining room. One of the upstairs floors has been raised slightly to give the dining room a higher ceiling.

The main feature of the living room is a low-level fireplace of volcanic stone. Other features include a low table made of oak and woven metal slats. The woven

theme is echoed in the bedroom, where woven oak wall paneling is reminiscent of Shaker design.

The overall impact of the apartment relies mainly on color and a combination of natural and artificial light. Despite the impression of rigidity and order, it feels so portable that it would take a mere few hours for Bonhotal to move out, leaving no trace save the warm but monastic shell.

CLASSICISM STRIPPED NAKED

Andrzej Zarzycki's Chelsea home in London, built in the 1860s, exudes a sense of purpose, demanding order, balance, and strict internal organization, despite the fact that it is not entirely symmetrical. It is a haven and focal point for the much-traveled designer, who describes it as "an expression of classicism, but a modern one, without all the trimmings. It is classicism stripped naked."

The generous four-story building, with its white stucco façade, represents a new order for the Zarzyckis. Andrzej, who is half Polish, grew up initially in Zambia, where he attended a Polish Catholic school. Then boarding school in England led him to study interior design, after which he joined forces with interiors supremo Anthony Collett, who is now his partner. Andrzej's wife Jill also grew up on the African continent.

Zarzycki admits to using "classically based principles, which are clearly about symmetry and hierarchy." The main rooms of the house work as pairs from front to back, making for ease of

BELOW Four chairs, a Brancusi-inspired table, a Danish cabinet, a lamp, a dramatic Lucio Fontana slit painting, and a collection of blown glass vases: the organization could not be simpler, yet the objects are refined in style and materials, and the proportions are just perfect. The same arrangement of different furniture could be as wrong as this is right. The ceiling lamp is by Zarzycki.

In this townhouse, ceiling moldings have been banished and symmetry reigns supreme. The more formal dining room upstairs, directly above the room for informal use (shown opposite), possesses greater refinement, along with the same sense of order. A red painting by Ian McKeever adds a slightly random note to the regimen of French mid-twentieth-century and modern pieces.

movement, and the rooms are partitioned not by doors but by sliding panels. Activity rooms front the tree-lined street, while rooms used primarily for repose overlook the backyard, itself a display of cultivated symmetry.

The ground floor and basement contain the kitchen—a large, quality affair decked in maple, with the best appliances—a couple of dens and an informal dining room with some exquisite Danish 1950s furniture. On the second floor are the formal dining and living rooms. The dining table and chairs are custom-designed by the Collett-Zarzycki partnership, while the console tables are classic French mid-twentieth-century. Paintings, including works by Lucio Fontana and Ian McKeever, are centrally placed on the walls throughout.

The house is now devoid of cornices and crown moldings, but some areas have been rethought with the addition of wall finishes such as burl elm and maple. The designer's attention to detail is evident in every door handle and cabinet-door hinge: "You cannot compromise on detail when stripping things away," maintains Zarzycki with insight.

"Elegance is refusal."

DIANA VREELAND, EDITOR OF AMERICAN VOGUE (1962–71)
AND CONSULTANT AT THE METROPOLITAN MUSEUM OF ART COSTUME INSTITUTE

ELEGANCE

The legendary fashion icon Diana Vreeland was perhaps unaware of how true her definition of elegance was to its original meaning: its roots are in the Latin word for to choose or select. I imagine she was referring to the refusal to be swayed by others, the refusal to abandon one's own predilections.

Vreeland was the epitome of twentieth-century classic and elegant yet personalized dressing. Her wardrobe was tailored in color and sentiment, but extensive nonetheless: she chose to wear mainly black and white with accents of red—her watch, worn on a fob, was poppy red. Peep into the closet of creative director of American *Vogue* Grace Coddington, and you will see an updated version: pairs of charcoal-gray flannel slacks beneath corresponding jackets, and flat shoes—thoroughly understated, almost gamine elegance.

It is impossible to create a "rendition" of elegance. The building blocks are not entirely definable, and their order, once established, is essential to the finished display. Take Vreeland again as an example. Her peculiar beauty and taste were born not of emulation of other people's ideas, but from a composite of all her previous experiences, which, duly "edited," manifested themselves as her own glorious personal attributes. Her memories were made from meeting and observing the bohemian set of the *belle époque.* Vreeland's formative years were spent in a socialite's Paris, where her hopelessly frivolous yet relatively impecunious parents introduced her to Nijinsky, Diaghilev, and Chaliapin. She saw Bernhardt and Duse perform, and studied ballet under Michel Fokine. Accomplishment was the other face of Vreeland's beauty.

Although her life was a far cry from that of English novelist Elizabeth Gaskell a century earlier, Vreeland would probably have agreed with Gaskell's comment that "economy was always 'elegant,' and money-spending always vulgar and ostentatious"—having spent years, as many of the most elegant people do, not quite having as much money as her peers. Sometimes, it seems, elegance finds its roots in necessity. The need to express oneself physically is an emotional issue. "Without emotion, there is no beauty," Vreeland once said.

The point of Gaskell's comment, of course, was to address the issue of fiscal restraint at a time when an outward display of wealth was considered to be a social faux pas. To my mind it still is. Suffice it to say that, in the world of interior design, it does not take money to create elegance, which has more to do with manners and making others comfortable. Elegance is synonymous with grace.

My own definition of elegance is something original but polished. It may be an old wooden floor, in which the polish fails to fill the cracks and the grain still stands clear, or an exquisite lacquered cabinet, with its sheerness and depth. Elegance is timeless, fastidious taste. Elegance is refusal—refusal to compromise.

BELOW A tailored dress is cut close to the body, but loose enough to allow movement. If the dress is too tight it cannot be elegant, according to the late Norman Mailer—speaking in reference to his friend Marilyn Monroe. Similarly, a streamlined room is in itself elegant. Here the bed is a generous size, and its duck's egg blue–satin cover, reminiscent of an Art Deco interior, has been tailored to fit, but with enough give to be luxurious.

DEFYING DEFINITION

"Elegance by default defies definition," asserts Yorkshire-born, science-trained interior designer Jonathan Reed. "It is something that happens, but cannot be created—the coming together of many elements in a non-scientific manner."

The graceful apartment created by Reed for his friends, fashion-design duo Alan Cleaver and Keith Varty, is a work of rare beauty and harmony that serves the clients' lifestyle and yet comprises a collection of disparate objects against a painterly background. Since Reed's work is made to order, his ethos is to avoid repetition. There is no Jonathan Reed "look," but a definite thread runs through all his highly textured work: quality, comfort, and artifice. Some of the pieces have no real value, save that of natural, indefinable refinement.

"My approach to Keith and Alan's apartment was to create a calm, comfortable studio or 'hotel suite,' with a great reception room for parties and dinners, tailored to the way they live while in London." The main aim, Reed explains, is to take the frenzy out of their lives: "to create a timeless space for people whose business follows a six-month cycle."

A late-Victorian conversion in one of London's garden squares, the apartment exudes elegance, not as a result of any one attribute, but thanks to an intuitive refinement and lightness of touch. Its bedroom-studio could be self-sufficient as a living space—there is a sofa area and a large architect's table in the window. The bed is recessed in a vellum-clad niche that separates it visually from the rest of

the room and whose neatness somehow finishes off preexisting plasterwork on the ceiling.

The vast room at the rear is perfect for entertaining, with comfortable seating in the center, taupe-fabric-covered Swedish Louis XV–style chairs on each side of the fireplace, and benches along one wall under a pair of pictures—an exercise in symmetry. More classic than the bedroom, this room creates the illusion of being in a larger townhouse. "New classics are like old classics—just with different colorations—a mix of comfort and practicality with a deep sense of luxury and a stroke of dramatic creativity," believes Reed.

ABOVE A variety of whites, this salon contains only freestanding furniture, each piece sculptural in form and balanced with the other elements in the room. The rectangular traveling case and square pillows and sofa contrast with the curvilinear eighteenth-century Italian urn, the pot, and the 1940s terracotta Italian lamp base, all of differing heights, materials, and textures. Vellum has been applied to the oak cabinet's face, evoking luxury and adding texture.

To be elegant, a room does not need riches. The occupants of this room spend limited time at each of their addresses, so simplicity is key. Items of disparate origins—some of great value, others purely of visual interest—are dispersed through their homes. The slate-topped, gilded-base console tables are by Reed Design; the painting is "after" Ben Nicholson—not an original, but its clarity, its square, and its circle unite the room.

The French 1940s period epitomizes
elegance: its furniture forms mimicked
Louis XVI style, just as those of the 1930s
had copied Louis XV—both of them
inspired by classical antiquity. The legs of
such mid-twentieth-century pieces are
among the most beautiful ever conceived:
some are zoomorphic, others turn outward,
while the straight ones end in a point, often
with a metal sabot at the bottom. The tea set
is also French.

BELOW Aparicio has a passion for form and, although stringent with clients' homes, is more free-fall in his own apartment, relying on his "eye" and his feeling for the pieces he assembles. Plinths or columns displaying empty vessels play a large part in his design.

BELOW The faded elegance of an old mirror that has lost some of its silver is a sophisticated addition above a superb desk. Too often it is assumed that furniture should be restored to perfection; although many craftspeople are capable of sensitive restoration, the patina of the past can be lovely. The *klismos* chair, a key form in ancient Greece and Rome that translated into the last century, is one of the most comfortable and beautiful shapes imaginable.

INSPIRED BY LATIN PASSION

In architect Carlos Aparicio's combined home and office, formerly two tiny apartments in a small townhouse a step away from the vibrant beat of Madison Avenue, the arrangement is much more Europe than New York. Rooms are strung out, one leading to another, like a Versailles corridor in miniature. None of the rooms is itself extraordinary; it is Aparicio's assemblages of exquisite furniture with various wall treatments that work the magic.

A protégé of Argentinian architects Machado and Silvetti, Aparicio studied at Rhode Island School of Design, then at Harvard. Despite this intellectual training, he is superstitious and intuitive. "My passion and mind are fighting all the time, but ultimately I react with my gut. My starting point is often a dream, but above all I like real things. Stucco is alive, it comes from minerals and has depth, and real things can only be elegant."

Aparicio was born in Cuba, but was forced to leave for Spain in 1966. Being in exile taught him how it feels to be displaced. For him, the work of some wartime designers has great significance: "A piece by Jean-Michel Frank is not only about his style, but also the beautiful, horrific story of his life as a Jew in exile. It is incredible his mind was producing serene things while his soul was so tormented."

Aparicio's rooms are packed with superlative furniture by mid-twentieth-century masters. His thinking goes beyond fashion: "It is not that we love the French 1940s, but that we recognize that objects created at that time are perfect in their classical proportions, materials, and simplicity." He seeks European pieces in Europe, where they retain a sense of context and are not mere commodities.

Notions of a single style are anathema to him, and he delights in surprising visitors by dancing salsa around his elegant rooms. "Your environment is key to your being; it really only matters that it is right for you. There is potential for any space, humble or grand."

SEAMLESS DESIGN

Interior architect Jackie Villevoye, one of the best designers in Europe, is blessed with a grand space—a large house in the Dutch town of Breda —and carte blanche on its design. The family lives in a double-fronted 1860 merchant's house that is a successful blend of form and content, and for that reason alone is elegant. Its interior decoration and architecture are seamless.

Like most houses of classical design, it displays symmetry throughout, and the rooms are well proportioned and suited to their use—Villevoye prefers to avoid multifunction rooms. There are three main floors and a basement.

Entry is into a grand central hallway with a black-and-white checkerboard floor in polished marble. Beyond a relatively minimalist library off the hall is the *pièce de résistance*, a new addition—an elongated dining room containing only a long table and dining chairs in different colors, most of them muted but some almost fuchsia. (The designer has added a single color to each monochrome room.) The lighting is subtle: at regular intervals along the walls, recessed full-length crevices house lights that are both up- and down-lighters. At the end, glass doors open onto a "French" garden of clipped topiary, so precise and elegant that the temptation to step outside is irresistible.

The main bedroom takes up the entire width of the house on the second floor and has a sizeable movie screen that slots into a box when not in use. Symmetrical seating includes a huge square taupe ottoman; taupe curtains lined in black taffeta provide blackout.

The Villevoye house demonstrates that principles of harmony and proportion can be adapted to extravagant or simple rooms. It also confirms Edith Wharton's view that "neither decoration nor furniture, however good of its kind, can look its best unless each is chosen with reference to the other."

An unadorned fireplace and chimney frame with empty mantel update a lofty living room. If the chimney were adorned with a painting, the effect would be too cluttered and the room would seem more vertical. This way, there is room for a collection of photographs, and the eye is drawn to the horizontal, creating a feeling of space. The contrasting "coffee" table in tobacco wood and low banquettes in pink also apparently draw the room down to a lower plane.

"*The state of emptiness I tried to achieve when I was twenty, a sort of disorientation which startles you out of sleep, is in my opinion connected with the idea of mental and visual comfort, more necessary than the anesthetizing effect of cozy surroundings.*"

ANDRÉE PUTMAN, FRENCH ENTREPRENEUR AND INTERIOR DESIGNER

COMFORT

When Andrée Putman was a child, her days divided between Paris, where she was "over-exposed" to art, and a lively country home, she read about the curious adventures of Patapouf and Filifer. Patapouf slept in a four-poster bed and, on awakening, would stretch out his hand to grasp one of many flavors of ice-cream dispensed by a machine next to his bed. In contrast, Filifer slept on the pipes of a stove, and when he awoke, a trapdoor opened automatically, sending him tumbling into a tub of iced water. According to Putman, she would rather be Patapouf for bathrooms, but Filifer for everything else!

Whether designing for hotels or private residences, the bathroom is Putman's first thought: it has to offer sanctuary. Another French design guru, Christian Liaigre, has a similar view. When Liaigre designed The Mercer hotel in New York, the bathrooms are said to have been his first priority: having constructed a pie-chart of how he imagined people spent their time while traveling, he concluded that they spent more hours sleeping, having sex, and bathing than anything else, and that his rooms should reflect this. Comfort, it seems, can stem from mathematics.

Comfort is not just about top-quality mattresses and soft pillows. It means having a sense of well-being, both physical and psychological, and its demands can be subtle and surprising. My eldest son has Asperger's Syndrome, or higher autism, as it is often dubbed. In the eight years I have been observing and serving him, Miles and the planet he lives on have taught me much about the comfort he requires as a person of augmented sensitivity. He needs both physical and mental comfort more than anything else in his life. As long as his furniture is the right size, fabrics do not irritate his skin, the colors around him are calm and harmonious, and he has enough space (people with Asperger's are not very spatially aware), he can lead the somewhat regimented, mathematical, and puzzle-solving life he enjoys so much, in orderly and soothing surroundings. Without these elements of visual and physical comfort, which translate into psychological wellbeing for him, his life descends into chaos.

Putman also has a passion for mathematics, as well as rhythm. "Geometry is the branch of mathematics concerned with space," she says. "Rhythm is the dimension of time that interrupts the orderliness of space." So it is rhythm, not a collection of tea cozies or plump, saggy armchairs, that gives us comfort in an orderly space. On furniture, she wonders whether it is "really so comfortable to allow things to become heavier and more unwieldy".

Ultimately, to be comfortable with something is to be confident in the correctness of your choice.

BELOW A chair to sit in, a lamp to read by, and a table upon which to place a glass: to be comfortable, a room must work. Humans are very sensitive to light, noise, and touch—even color schemes can affect how we feel about our environment and ourselves. For a chair to be comfortable, it must be firm enough to support the sitter, but soft enough, unless it is a dining or desk chair, to relax in. Above all, it must have the right pitch, the right degree of comfort and support in ergonomic terms.

RIGHT In the library-spare room, a bed is covered with a custom-made coverlet and skirt in mohair velvet. These belie its usual function and make it a comfortable lounging area for reading. There are many surprising elements here: the Eames chair is in the original brown wool, the table is French 1930s, and the lamp has a crystal stem. The painting of a matador who died in the ring is by Angelo Ponce de Leon, a cousin of the King of Spain. The bookcases are French military office cabinets.

ABOVE In the living room, a pair of huge armchairs designed by Basham for his own needs hold court. Large chairs are omnipresent in comfortable chic interiors. It is said that a three-seater sofa rarely has a person sitting in its center; since few of us have room for a four-seater, the best option is for a pair of two-seater sofas or a pair of voluminous chairs. The spears are African.

CREATURE COMFORTS

Never was this more so that in the apartment of Nye Basham, an American in Paris. Happy to think of himself as a "decorator" and aesthete, Basham went to Paris to work for Ralph Lauren in the 1980s and never looked back. He now runs his own business from home, where he plans and designs as well as relaxing and entertaining.

Although many of his projects involve the reapportioning of space, Basham's own home remains true to its original form. It is a petit-bourgeois apartment of medium proportions that has good bones and enough architectural detail—plasterwork, ceiling and crown moldings, and architraves—to remind him that he is as central as can be in Paris, with views of the Garnier Opera House and a short walk to the Palais Royal.

Yet fine French furniture of the eighteenth and nineteenth centuries, the obvious choice for many Parisians, is considered

unimaginative by Basham, unless it is mixed with other periods. "Also, it is not easy to sit on a Louis XVI chair for more than a few minutes," he points out. "The most interesting French period was the 1930s and '40s. It has the best of both worlds: the craftsmanship and ease of the twentieth century, and the delicacy and period placement of centuries past."

This decorator uses all manner of ingredients. His art collection contains *objets trouvés* hung with

such aplomb that one is reluctant to ask about their provenance. And he is a master of artifice. In a spare bedroom which doubles as a library, a double bed is dressed with a heavy quilted-velvet fitted covering that certainly does not evoke "bedroom."

In the salon, large gray armchairs support cushions in magenta, coral, and celadon velvet. One of the most comforting aspects of this home is the harmonious color scheme and sophisticated palette.

ABOVE A pair of Egyptian stools made in Cairo—styled after stools found in King Tutankhamen's tomb in the 1920s—double as side tables and are a practical addition to the other side table, a re-edition of a rare piece by Jacques Adnet in oak and bronze, by Adnet's daughter. The art is a war shield from Papua New Guinea; the 1950s chair in oak came from a Los Angeles hotel.

In this living room, comfort is assured by the pair of sofas by Christian Liaigre, from a collection distributed in the United States by Holly Hunt, along with Liaigre's other designs. The sofas also serve to balance the graphic quality of the wall-hung sculpture that dominates the room. The pair of benches at the end of the coffee table, themselves artworks, are by Bruno Romeda.

BLENDING GEOMETRY Design impresario Holly Hunt found herself at a crossroads in her life when all her children had left home. Her charming and rather large family house was no longer appropriate to her needs, and although she still required the same level of comfort that she had become used to, Hunt felt it was time for a change—but was not attracted to the lofts and "interesting" bohemian spaces of downtown Chicago.

The architectural genius of her former house was a hard act to follow. It had been designed by the prestigious firm Perkins, Fellows and Hamilton in 1915, a time of boom in Chicago, which possesses some of the world's best early-twentieth-century architecture (and is the home of the American skyscraper, thanks to architect Louis Sullivan, mentor of Frank Lloyd Wright). Hunt eventually acquired a superlative apartment on the pre-eminent East Lake Shore Drive, with astounding lake views.

On one of the upper floors of a building designed by renowned architect Benjamin Marshall, her home is a divine purpose-built apartment that is bathed in light and possesses all its original features. The enfilade of rooms from front to back includes a living room, a dining room behind glass-paned doors, and an orangery. On the opposite axis, three bedrooms swing to the left, and supporting rooms, including a kitchen, to the right. In many American cities, home design is preoccupied with the latest trends. Chicago, in the heart of the country, is different: here domestic design seems more firmly rooted, less erratic, and destined to last.

New pieces of furniture designed by Hunt, Christian Liaigre (whose work Hunt introduced to the United States), and Frenchman Christian Astuguevieille, together

ABOVE Throughout, furniture echoes the geometry of the art, a psychologically comforting exercise. The colorful work by British artist Howard Hodgkin adds accent color to a muted palette, as does much of the art. Hunt was drawn to the openness of the apartment, which enables it comfortably to support the dramatic nature of her art collection.

BELOW In the window of the master bedroom overlooking the lake, a step creates a separate area for repose, television, and reading. The linen-covered and sublimely elegant pair of chairs—my personal favorite, for both appearance and comfort—are by Antonio Citterio for B&B Italia.

with a mahogany piece by Chicago-based artist Hans van der Hill, blend easily with the original classical features. Hunt had the opportunity to custom-design many elements, which look as if they have been there forever, including the linen chair slipcovers in the orangery and the linen-and-silk carpets. The tailored furniture throughout echoes reassuringly the geometry of the art collection—the Motherwells, a Frankenthaler, a Nevelson, a Rauschenberg, and a de Kooning. "I have always been drawn to abstract expressionism," says Hunt. "It is comfortable and warm and not too minimalist."

OPEN TO NATURE

"Even though it possesses drama, there is nothing formal about this house," says interior designer Ted Russell, who lives with portrait photographer Matthew Rolston in a Beverly Hills home designed by the architect Richard Neutra in 1961. Despite its dramatic potential, on a mountaintop with panoramic views, the house has not been treated as a shrine to its eminent architect, but has been personalized with an enviable and eclectic collection of furniture and objects. True to the architect's ethos, it is a comfortable, down-to-earth home that eschews preciousness.

Neutra was an Austrian who immigrated in 1923 to the West Coast, where he played a significant role in the development of modern architecture. From Europe he brought vigor and precision; in America he developed a more human and poetic form. His houses are almost transparent in places, with frameless mitered window joints (a device pioneered by Frank Lloyd Wright). Sheet glass dominates, allowing large amounts of soft daylight to illuminate spaces created by dispensing with interior walls. The natural world outside becomes part of the space: access to sunlight, views, and exterior design are key. It was for extending the concept of open-plan beyond the house itself that Neutra became known—a less heroic version of Frank Lloyd Wright.

This house is a distillation of Modernism, with clean lines, post-and-beam construction, and open-plan living, but has no harshness. Single-story, it extends in an L shape around the pool, with the bedroom and living room in a separate "wing" from the activity rooms. It is a perfect example of good circulation: each room can be entered from the pool terrace or from another room.

The color palette is essentially neutral, with bright accents. Texture is abundant: glossy leathers, animal skins, and grainy woods against surfaces such as French limestone. For all its architectural dynamism, this is a soothing, livable home.

ABOVE A sliding mirrored door closes off the bedroom from the living room for privacy in the otherwise open floor plan. The cerused oak sleigh bed and the desk (seen in reflection) in the master bedroom are by Michael Berman. Sumptuous bed sheets and covers are very enticing, as is the accessibility of the pool and terrace, via window walls. Ease of movement is key.

"This same thing does the divine voice hear, thunder, repeat: Da! Da! Da! That is, restrain yourselves, give, be compassionate. One should practice this same triad...."

THE UPANISHADS, SANSKRIT SACRED BOOKS (CIRCA 400–200 B.C.)

RESTRAINT

Throughout the twentieth and at the start of the twenty-first century, whenever new forms and theories of architecture have come into being, there has been a strong correlation between restraint and compassion. To apply restraint need not mean being ascetic or holding back emotion—on the contrary, it often requires empathy—but it does mean adhering to principles that make sense for building practice and for those living in the buildings. A functional approach does not need to be unimaginative, inelegant, or harsh: the best examples are celebrated for their integrity, true classics of modernity.

We have lost sight somewhat of the original principles of Modernist architecture, its social conscience. In most urban areas today, the only inhabitants of intentionally minimalist and "utilitarian" spaces are those who have employed architects to create them, but I know of a few classic modern apartments in London where painstaking attention to detail and a vast budget have gone into the restoration of homes originally built for the common man; and rightly so, since they are of historic interest and should be maintained. One is in a building in Notting Hill by Walter Gropius, where two small apartments have been converted into one three-bedroomed unit, and another is the north London penthouse Russian émigré Berthold Lubetkin built for himself in the 1930s atop Highpoint Two, commissioned by the Hungarian Gestetner family as a high-rise building for their workforce.

Many architects and construction companies in the early twentieth century were attempting to solve the housing shortage resulting from wartime destruction by creating smaller houses as prototypes. The Bauhaus architects in Germany (led by Gropius and Mies van der Rohe), the Constructivists in Russia, Eileen Gray and Le Corbusier in France, all worked to produce simplified "machines for living in." Once the forms were devised, standardization became the great battle cry, the aim being ease and efficiency for those inhabiting the spaces and for the architects designing them. The Modernists designed components for mass-production—including prefabricated wall panels, windows, even doors—and generally moved the construction world increasingly toward industrialization.

Irish-born Eileen Gray, who built her own home in the south of France, was also guided by principles of human need. She demanded that "the interior plan should not be an incidental result of the façade," and the house's inhabitants should each be able, if need be, to "find total independence and an atmosphere of solitude and concentration."

But the man whose manifesto we most value when dissecting the "restraints" of Modernism is Le Corbusier. In 1926, he reduced his principles of architecture to a basic five. The perfect house stands on supporting columns, or *pilotis*; has a roof reached by a staircase; is open-plan, with both free-standing and attached walls; has horizontally orientated windows; and, last but by no means least, has a large south-facing window (north-facing if in the southern hemisphere) that creates an opening façade.

Many restrained Modernists have found inspiration in India, particularly in the simple symmetry of thousand-year-old Jainist temples. Le Corbusier worked in India on a number of major projects, but curiously there was much less feeling for his ethos at home, and neither the United States nor France offered him major public works to design. Perhaps the ancient principles of restraint were too revolutionary.

BELOW A minimalist interior is not an interior stripped naked, an empty box: to be successful, it requires almost more thought than any other kind. Here the architect wanted to leave the ceiling exposed, as well as some of the brick, but the walls were drywalled for refinement and in most places floated several inches from the brick (making it possible to uplight from behind). He wanted to float the ceiling, too, so uplighting was installed behind the gypsum-board walls. In the dining-room portion of this vast urban living space, the chairs and table are dwarfed by the vast scale, yet the interior's ethereal nature means that, although spartan and devoid of embellishment, it is not sterile.

EXPLORATION OF SPACE

When Susan and Paul Zucker commissioned the famously stringent architect Larry Booth to convert a 3,200-square-foot (300-square-meter) ruin, they were under no illusions. According to Paul, a property developer, "There was nothing romantic about this building." The couple wanted to explore the form of the massive space, giving it a sense of orientation by using building rather than decorative materials; not over-domesticating it, but honoring its "commercial muscularity" with all the integrity of Modernist principles.

The brick building had been the boiler house of a meat-processing business in Chicago's less-than-glamorous South Lakeview district. Now it occupies 8,200 square feet (760 square meters) and exhibits

Palladian geometry: windows and doors mirror one another from room to room and from inside to outside. Poured concrete was laid in oversized slabs as a floor, and what was once a parking lot has become the kitchen wing (which also includes a TV-viewing and general leisure area).

The bulk of the ground floor comprises the vast living area, its scale reminiscent of a medieval banqueting hall. A formal dining room, part of this main space, could not be more pared-down, containing only two square, glass-topped tables and ranks of white leather-covered chairs. A floating wall conceals a small second kitchen. Upstairs, three bedrooms, four bathrooms, and a gym (plus an outdoor "deck"), though sizeable, are dwarfed by a 40-foot (12-meter) pool visible through a glass wall in the master bathroom.

Rather than thinking about how to fill rooms, the Zuckers were more concerned with spaces as shapes. They wanted to be able to look from the front door through to the trapezoidal backyard. This front-to-back line became the major axis. The second axis is perpendicular to the entrance and to its right, leading through the colonnaded living and dining area to an office.

The Zucker residence is an exploration of space, vision, and harmony. As Booth explains, "The geometry gives you a sense of balance and order: the axes lead you gently from place to place." Despite the spartan appearance, it evokes serenity and comfort.

LEFT In the dining area, eight substantial chairs and a specially commissioned table in two pieces stand in front of a floating wall, behind which is the support kitchenette that assists the massive main kitchen when guests come. The house is a paean to minimalism and yet comfortably embracing.

ABOVE The main living area contains this floor-to-ceiling fireplace—steel sheeting over a frame box—which pays homage to the inherent strength of the building, echoed most effectively in stark form. Windows and doors are positioned symmetrically in the principal rooms, and skylights throughout fall on the fenestration grids. It was when the architect saw the cement-beamed ceiling that he fell in love with the property and decided to take on the project. The furnishings, essentially European, include a lengthy sofa by B&B Italia and a pair of chairs by Philippe Starck.

BELOW Despite the interior's overall restraint, Putman has allowed room for De Poortere to display a "self-portrait" of fine objects, including bronze sculptures by Lynn Chadwick, brasswork by Michel Berrocal, egg shapes by Lucio Fontana, a figured head by Max Ernst, and a tiny Henry Moore piece. The iron side table, one of a pair, is by Pierre Chareau.

CALM NEUTRALITY When

redesigning the small penthouse apartment of art collector Patrick De Poortere, Andrée Putman's aim was to enhance the art and distill its owner's ideas on collecting: "He grew up in a large house crammed with collections, surrounded by vestiges of the past. I had the same feeling about my early homes and the need to go back to a blank page. Sometimes this profession is more psychoanalysis than design," she says. Putman made her debut in the early 1960s as a stylist with French magazines L'Oeil and Femina.

Her first house was for Michel Guy, later French Minister of Culture.

De Poortere's apartment is in a 1970s seafront building at Knokke-Le-Zoute in Belgium. "I liked the hues of sea and sky, and brought them inside to create serenity," says Putman. Flattering to art and sculpture, the muted colors were also inspired by museums, where "the environment lets what is displayed speak for itself." Nothing is on show that should not be, and clothes are hidden in ingenious pullout closets in the bathroom. Structural alterations were made to

maximize natural light: walls wrapped around a central courtyard acquired large windows, and a sight-line was created from the northern sea-facing terrace to the sun-warmed south terrace. The apartment is mainly open-plan, with sliding sanded-glass doors and copper-mesh screens that allow air through and create shadow play.

For Putman, function being paramount, the bathroom is vital (see page 26). This apartment has a large one; its electric-blue washbasin of volcanic rock, together with a midnight-blue

BELOW The designer created a recessed horizontal lamp in the headboard, which also acts as a bedside table. Push-buttons not only illuminate various recessed lights in the bedroom and bathroom, but open the electric blinds so the view over the town can be seen without having to leave the bed. The monastic room supports one small painting by a friend, Frank Ver Elst.

banquette in the dining niche, are the only concessions to true color.

Most impressive is the precision. In the showers, for example, tiny mirrored tiles at eye level fit snugly without having been cut. Respect for mathematical pattern and discipline, acquired as a student of music, inspires Putman's designs.

RIGHT "The apartment works very precisely, like a clock," says Putman: she imposed restraint in order to clear the mind of its occupant, who had lived his life with paraphernalia. Bleached teak panels in the bedroom, concealing storage, continue into the bathroom, which features the only remaining support pillar in the apartment.

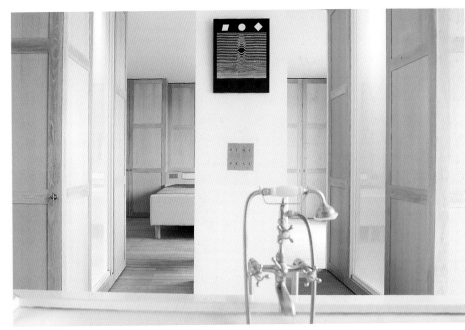

"All my life... fate has somehow led me to the climax of other people's dramas."

MIKHAIL LERMONTOV, NINETEENTH-CENTURY RUSSIAN WRITER, FROM *A HERO OF OUR TIMES*

DRAMA

The history of drama—in interior design as much as on the stage—is largely a history of changing dramatic values. In the theater, the presentation of thought gradually became as important as the representation of emotion, which had initially been the main element. At the beginning of the twentieth century, according to actor and playwright H. Granville-Barker, "Plays grew so austerely intellectual that their performance seemed a profanation, and we saw the actors moving apologetically through their parts as if they had been told they were rather vulgar people." Drama had lost its original meaning of "a thing done" (a translation from the Greek) and become something much more deliberate. As spectators of interior design, we do not generally expect the dramatic interior to provoke thought rather than emotion, and yet a great deal of thought may have gone into it.

True drama consists of emotions, opinions, and occurrences presented in three dimensions; the dramatic interior is no exception. It must exhibit its own confidence as well as the confidence, emotions, and opinions of those who choose to live in it. Dramatic homes are not for the fainthearted, especially as they frequently play host to a critical audience. Some of the objects and expressions within are larger than life and beg curiosity.

According to the Greek philosopher Aristotle in his *Poetics*, the three considerations when creating drama are the unifying threads of time, place, and action, which for decorative purposes can be translated as period, space, and function. A dramatic room can be taken from any period, but it generally needs to be on a grander scale than most, or at least to appear to be so. Aristotle observed that "imitation is natural to man from childhood.... And it is also natural for all to delight in works of imitation." It is natural to be curious about other settings, places beyond one's wildest imagination, and there is nothing wrong with emulation, as long as you do your homework or take professional advice. It is perfectly acceptable to re-create the splendors of a classical Roman bath house, for example, given enough space and the right materials.

Most modern drama, in contrast to classical theater, is self-avowedly entertainment, intended for our delight. A modern dramatic interior gives free rein to the imagination, and is achievable in a smaller space than is often thought, especially if it is personality-driven.

When a designer creates a dramatic stage for other people's lives, they become a conduit for expression, encouraging the occupants to abandon any reservation or reticence, and breathing new life into their sense of fantasy. Successful dramatic interiors must not be manipulated by the architect or designer to accommodate their own personal whims; rather the designer's task is to dress things up here, dress them down there, but generally make sure that the drama is that of the occupants themselves. Those wishing to make a dramatic statement must be prepared to take center stage.

BELOW In a dramatic home a sense of theater prevails: rich tones and deep-pile fabrics, both plain and patterned, combined with sound architecture as a backdrop, enhance the contrasts and relationship between objects and furniture. A home can be viewed as a cinematographic masterpiece, where one scene flows from another, where each room billows and blooms in anticipation of the next. In a classic home, all elements have to be carefully considered—and as Mies van der Rohe observed in *The New York Times* in 1969, "God is in the details."

RIGHT The selection of furniture is a modern interpretation of how a home would have been in the nineteenth century—it would not have been "decorated" at speed, but evolved over decades. European antiques, French and English particularly, restored and recovered in the finest of new fabrics so as not to look musty, and carefully selected oddities blend with Asian and other art. Each piece has its value, even if its provenance is not always entirely clear.

ABOVE In an Italianate house of nineteenth-century elegance and proportion, on a corner of two very fine streets, the depth has been augmented by opening up the two principal rooms on the second floor, between which lies the mouth of a grand staircase. The French Empire-style mirror above the fireplace was created to match one in the living room beyond. The owner likes substantial antiques that are not overly ornamental, such as the Georgian English klismos chair.

PERIOD DRAMA In the late-nineteenth-century New York depicted by novelist Henry James, characters sashayed from one grand house to another, the *mise en scène* meticulously described. James reflected faithfully the society he observed, his subjects coming from a leisured class for whom life appeared naturally as a work of art. In a recent restoration in New York, Stephen Sills and James Huniford showed similar objectivity while acknowledging the level of drama their client would appreciate.

It is rare to find a house from this period that retains its volume, singularity, and beauty; rarer still to find a gem, in a corner location near Gramercy Park, the literary epicenter of New York City, that has been remodeled and yet holds true to its period. The present owner had the foresight to approach Europhile interior designers Sills and Huniford, who have immersed themselves in the history of art

and furniture, and for whom boldness and subtlety are one.

Built in 1854, the house stands four storys tall. Entry is into a single vast space—a games-room-den-repose-room—with a floor of bleached oak and inserted slabs of brown slate. Plaster dentil crown moldings adorn the walls in *stucco de Venezia*.

A newly built staircase salutes the second floor, another open space with separate areas defined by pillars and beams. A large Arts and Crafts carpet in jewel colors, found in London, accessorizes the floor. The highly polished mahogany dining table is from the era of Louis Philippe, while the chairs are Charles X—antiques that are not too fragile or valuable, but attractive and bold all the same.

The colors and mood become lighter as one moves toward the top of the house. In the bedrooms, canopied beds create "rooms within rooms"; in the master bedroom there are eight window panels overlooking the city.

The house now confidently reflects the grandeur of mid-nineteenth-century Manhattan, with all the European influences fashionable at that time. Its resultant atmosphere and textures are heightened by the theatrical play of daylight and shadow achieved within its walls.

ABOVE A daring combination of dark and brilliant hues makes the rooms appear larger. The furniture could have been family pieces handed down or picked up on travels. Seventeenth-century Chinese prints (a set of twelve, plus two new ones created by the designers) line the living-room walls. The draperies are copper-colored cotton-rayon mix, the blinds nineteenth-century Japanese cane, their seams covered with strips of silk from an antique obi or kimono sash.

BELOW Scale is the key. It is the drama of the art that draws the eye in this formerly Spanish-hacienda-style house, now a reapportioned blend of Modernist and classical. Far from matching her art to her home, Lewis purchased the house primarily because its ceilings were potentially high enough to accommodate her larger art pieces.

CUTTING A DASH
Sally Sirkin Lewis cuts a dramatic figure: in her dress, her early inspiration having been couture; in her decision-making—"I would sooner do without than make a compromise"; and in the statements made by her interiors. She has reigned in fabric, furniture, and interior design for almost half a century (she began her career in the late 1950s), and holds steadfast to the belief that good design, whether in couture or interiors, never goes out of fashion.

For her first house commission, at the age of twenty, Lewis mixed the paints herself. This was the genesis of the neutral palette for which she became renowned as the "beige lady," and the basis for the textile collections produced under her J. Robert Scott label—thousands of textiles and hundreds of chairs, sofas, ottomans, tables, lights, beds, and accessories. Many of her chair designs have been patented; they are often inspired by period chairs, reinterpreted by altering the scale. One of her signature materials is Lucite, a clear plastic out of vogue up to the 1960s. Lewis made it a classic, and almost invisible curved tables adorn her home. Textures also matter to her: "They are my patterns." Linen-lined walls, perfectly seamed, form a backdrop in the bedrooms. Another signature is zebra skin.

Lewis's home in Los Angeles is her sanctuary, its tone set by an art collection that includes works by Jean Arp, Milton Avery, and Robert Motherwell. The ceiling in the salon was raised to take an Adolph Gottlieb painting 8 feet (2.4 meters) tall, *Pink Smash* (1959). "Scale, proportion and color have to say something together," she says. "There has to be unity and balance to yield serenity and strength."

BELOW Lewis's innovative combinations of zebra motif, ethnic and ancient artifacts, and contemporary furnishings set a new standard of dramatic elegance for today's lifestyle. Her reputation rests on her unerring eye and uncompromising standards, neutral color palette and juxtaposition of textures. "I apply fashion techniques to furniture," she explains.

A TOTAL WORK OF ART

"A dynamic urban view, generous light and high ceilings" was what interior designer Terry Hunziker was looking for in downtown Seattle in the mid-1990s. The city itself possesses a sense of drama—not only in the surrounding natural beauty, its waters, and its heritage, but also as a thriving, fast-moving, and extremely prosperous industrial center.

What he found were two adjoining apartments in a red-brick building from about 1900 that had once been a hotel. They were on two levels: a larger lower level and a smaller upper level opening on to a deck or terrace—another of his prerequisites. First of all he gutted them, then dramatically transformed the space, boldly creating a truly modern and multi-faceted classic apartment. The view is magnificent, and even the sound of leaves invades at the right pitch.

Hunziker believes that texture provides not just the backdrop, but the essence of a space: "An apartment is successful if the surfaces provide interest." In this case the surfaces include industrial finishes and effects that invoke the impression of a factory or loft space. Despite its two levels, the apartment has a loft-like feel: downstairs the space has been reapportioned using floating walls and other clever devices such as subtle changes in color and wall textures—metal and high-gloss car paints are counterbalanced by hand-troweled plaster—to make the eye wander. To avoid walls outlining spaces conventionally and doors needing to be opened and walked through, Hunziker uses free-floating planes to suggest rooms; many touch neither floor nor ceiling, but stand away with a reveal or gap.

There are no real hallways in the apartment, just the suggestion of them by way of steel runners embedded in the floor, to distinguish one part from another. In other areas, maple alongside concrete on the floor is echoed on the ceiling. The cleverest device, however, is a horizon line running along many of the walls, a unifying element that doubles as a display shelf—subtle and at the same time deeply dramatic.

ABOVE The scrap-metal screen was designed by Hunziker and David Gulassa. In places Hunziker used car paint in dull shades to lend a sheen to walls—the automotive lacquer was inspired, rather prosaically, by his own car. "I use a lot of metal, industrial paints, and materials in my work," he says, combining this, in confident polyglot manner, with early-nineteenth-century Russian and other European antiques, particularly Germanic, and mid-twentieth-century pieces including a plywood chair by Alvar Aalto.

RIGHT The polished concrete in the entrance hall leads to clear-coated maple in the gallery and dining area, echoed on the ceiling. A tray table, sitting against a wall between two long windows, is one of Hunziker's most cherished pieces; it was made by Gio Ponti in collaboration with Piero Fornasetti. Photography proliferates.

Following modern strategies rather than standard neoclassicism, this interior is a hymn to twenty-first-century mobility. A clean, contemporary apartment need not be sterile: here fireplaces—this one in volcanic rock—have been pared down to a functional minimum, and walls textured and toned to raise the spiritual temperature. Oak is used throughout, and each piece of furniture is carefully chosen or custom-designed to create a unified, flexible whole.

PRINCIPLES

The genesis of a truly elegant interior begins with certain principles, guiding such aspects as architectural form, lighting, color, texture, and shapes. These principles have developed out of the experience of solving design problems, but none are hard-and-fast rules, and there is no need to adhere to conventional solutions where original ideas offer inspiration; once started along sound lines, a room needs only to develop its magic.

ARCHITECTURE AND SPACE

"Simplicity, suitability, and proportion" were the watchwords of Edith Wharton, the American gentlewoman widely regarded as the world's first interior designer, or at least interior-design expert. In a classic, chic interior, these are probably the most fundamental elements: the proportions of the architecture set the tone for everything else and—while, of course, adjustments can be made—an interior that works is one that suits its structure and spaces as much as it does its inhabitants.

Edith Wharton crystallized her design philosophy in *The Decoration of Houses*, published in 1897 in collaboration with the architect Ogden Codman, Junior, and the later *Italian Villas and their Gardens*, published in 1904, lavishly illustrated by Maxfield Parrish. Wharton is best known as a novelist—a chronicler of late-nineteenth-century and early-twentieth-century social mores, she was the first woman to win the

Pulitzer Prize for literature—but equally significant are her invention of the concept of interior design and her understanding of architecture and space.

In *The Decoration of Houses*, Codman and Wharton sought to catapult the notion of interior design as a profession into the public consciousness. Codman was interested in classical styles, while Wharton had been impressed by the architects Charles Follen McKim (a graduate of Paris's Ecole des Beaux-Arts and part of a team responsible for the grand interiors of the Boston Public Library and the Pierpont Morgan Library in New York) and Stanford White (New York's leading Beaux-Arts architect), both of whom pioneered a close working relationship between architects and designers of the interior. This issue is still under discussion today; interior designers are often, I think mistakenly, deemed the interlopers of the profession.

In their manifesto claiming "house decoration as a branch of architecture," the prescient Wharton and Codman urged both architects and decorators to pay heed to the spatial consequences of decorative decisions, and to allow themselves to be guided by common sense and a respect for simplicity. They believed that for too long people had been building up gaudy ornamentation and superficial effects in their homes.

The resonance of these teachings reverberated throughout the twentieth century, and "simplicity, suitability, and proportion" remain the three key elements to take into account when considering architecture and space. If a room works well, it often looks good: functionality and appearance nurture each other, as in the Roman maxim "a healthy mind in a healthy body"—an appropriate echo of classical thought, given the role of neoclassicism in much of the best interior design.

LEFT The home of interior designer Daniel Romualdez on Manhattan's East Side perfectly exemplifies neoclassical symmetry and proportion, echoing the classical Roman combination of Greek decoration with Roman structurally efficient concrete. "Leaded" windows, their northerly light gently breathing life into the double-height room, are original to the building. French Empire and Directoire inflections and heavy nineteenth-century Baltic *klismos* chairs finish the classicism to perfection.

BELOW Overlooking the Parc Monceau in Paris, this duplex apartment exudes simplicity. All interior embellishments were removed in the 1930s, so the current owner began with a blank canvas. Formerly three separate apartments in a mid-nineteenth-century mansion—two on one floor and one on another—the newly created space nonetheless exhibits good circulation.

ABOVE "There is probably not an ugly room in France. In America you have to create the room that in Europe already exists," says designer Stephen Sills. Apart from its decorative moldings, this Paris apartment, the creation of another American decorator, Nye Basham, exemplifies the architectural features that are so important to the success of a room: natural good proportions, grace, and balance. The dining-room chairs are part of a set of twelve by Jacques Quinet, unearthed by Yves Gastou.

REAPPORTIONING SPACES

Many kinds of architecture can support a classic interior: the essential starting point is a home of good proportions, whether grand or modest. Well-proportioned structures may, of course, be formal houses, such as Federal and British Georgian buildings (architecture from the late eighteenth century) and some Victorian houses, but they may also be less formal, for instance, ranch houses, single-story dwellings, or split-level houses and cottages. Latterly, there have been even less formal yet chic homes in the form of loft and warehouse dwellings—industrial units adapted for housing, many of which have been gentrified and made to look very chic indeed. No matter how grand or diminutive, all of the above can be elegant, provided there is a little thought about how to live and an eye to the abandonment of clutter and the relationship between well-chosen objects within the space. As interior designer Ann Boyd once remarked, it is not only the objects themselves that help to create a balanced interior, but the mass of the void between them.

Given a classic building, there is scope for alteration and modernization without jeopardizing its inherent elegance, so long as it is reapportioned appropriately. Traditionally, a town house of several storys used as a main residence would have had not only ample space, but also staff to match, a luxury beyond most people's means in the twenty-first century. When these houses were built, enormous kitchens were designed to be in the basement or semi-basement, alongside the quarters for the "below stairs" staff. Dining rooms, drawing rooms, and parlors were on first and second floors, with bedrooms upstairs.

ABOVE, FAR LEFT This Seattle loft has been transformed with shifting planes and contrasting textures. The existing windows were not very tall, and the section at the base is blocked by brickwork: these factors have been countered by building out the surrounding walls to create the illusion that the windows are taller and narrower, and installing steel French doors with frosted glass at the bottom to conceal the brick. The upholstered chair, one of a pair, is a reproduction by Thomas Lamb of a 1930s piece.

ABOVE, LEFT A chic, diminutive rowhouse, a "workman's" cottage in London's East End, has a room on each of its three levels—ground, half-landing, and upper floors. Art impresario Maureen Paley uses the half-landing level at the rear as her dining area: the kitchen neatly takes up a small section of the room. The candelabra on the table is eighteenth-century.

ABOVE The Zucker residence in Chicago was created around a vast abandoned factory built between 1920 and 1940. The 3,200-square-foot (300-square-meter) single-story brick ruin became the nucleus of a 8,200-square-foot (760-square-meter) home and office on two floors. The vast kitchen and den, seen here, has been built on what used to be the parking lot, with windows on two sides. Doors to the right lead to the main space.

ABOVE, RIGHT In this Westminster apartment, home to Winston Churchill in the 1930s and later to Svetlana Stalin, the principal floor has been reapportioned to create an enfilade of rooms with a corridor running parallel. Two sets of partition doors open up the space for entertaining. Other doors give on to the hall from each section of the gallery, so that the three rooms, originally separate, can be used individually. A dramatic art collection includes pieces by Langlands and Bell, whose works the owners collect avidly.

The topmost small rooms were used as accommodation for chambermaids and staff looking after the children. These houses functioned very satisfactorily in machinelike manner in the eighteenth and nineteenth centuries; the staff were omnipresent, but privacy was attainable.

Today, even a house of these proportions is not easy for a family to occupy unless the room functions are rethought. For example, a host would rather be able to dart in and out of a social event in his own home, and cook in an adjoining room, than be banished to a lower floor for the first hour or so, during which the tone for the whole occasion may be set. It is just not practical to entertain and prepare a meal on two separate floors, and quite impossible to negotiate takeout cartons and packaging within elegant dining areas (home delivery of food being so popular

these days); the simplest solution is to have a kitchen and dining room adjacent to one another or, in a smaller space, a galley or "ship's" kitchen as part of a dining/living room. Architect and gallery owner Carlos Aparicio (*see* pages 22–23) has even gone so far as to eliminate the kitchen entirely from his New York apartment in favor of a single clean counter-top, almost a shelf, built into a niche in a corridor between two rooms, since he almost exclusively dines out. His only cooking apparatus is a top-notch coffeemaker.

In contrast, at the Zucker residence in Chicago designed by architect Larry Booth (*see* pages 36–37), a former factory that has undergone complete reapportioning, the owners specified the need for an enormous kitchen, fully equipped with all elements traditionally found in other areas of the house, since this is the heart of the voluminous building, where the couple entertains, lavishly yet informally: the focal point of the room is a massive built-in television screen for sports viewing. The main loft-type ground-floor space is adjacent to the kitchen, and comprises living and formal dining areas devoid of any embellishment at all; concealed behind a floating wall is a second kitchen area which secretly and demurely serves the dining room.

Adaptations to a home to suit the personality and modern-day needs of its dwellers must be in keeping both with the character of the building itself and with its inhabitants' pattern for living—although, as they grow, as tastes and situations change, they may develop a new blueprint. Obviously, a family of six would be unlikely to feel at ease in an open-plan multi-thousand-square-foot loft dwelling, but a solitary single person or a couple might. It would make more sense for a family to live in a house where stairs and halls can subdivide living spaces, for privacy. Conversely, there would be little point in a childless couple living in a five-story house where perhaps the upper three floors would see the light of day only when guests needed a bed.

LEFT A niche off a corridor in this apartment has been used to full advantage to make a comfortable reading and lounging area. It would have been easy to make the mistake of placing a credenza or substantial piece of furniture here, since we often take the cue to "fill" a space—rather like the mystifying handbag principle (it has always astounded me that women fill their handbags, no matter what the size, and whether or not they need all the items).

ABOVE The neatness of the dining table and its contrasting textures create a feeling of compartmentalization, despite the fact that there are no walls to divide the living, gallery, and dining spaces in a home where free-floating planes suggest rooms rather than define them concretely. Terry Hunziker designed the table in quarter-sawn white oak veneer and steel. The Russian birchwood chairs are circa 1815. The niche containing the shelf is echoed at the far end of the room.

ABOVE It is rare for a townhouse to be converted successfully into apartments, and although many property developers are now sensitive to the desirability of retaining and restoring original architectural features, little thought is given to the person who has to inhabit rooms of imperfect proportions for their functions. Jonathan Reed has succeeded in working around some original features in this client's home to devise a clear-cut, modern, symmetrical bed niche in a multipurpose room.

A good home is one that works. It does not necessarily have to follow the principles set out by Modernism's most influential architect, Swiss-born Charles-Edouard Jeanneret, known as Le Corbusier, who proclaimed his determination to create "a machine for living in," and whose heroes were engineers. Nor does it need to be, as promoted by America's Cranbrook Academy's first president Eliel Saarinen, a "total work of art" where a single aesthetic consciousness determines the look of everything, from the art on the walls to the jewelry worn by the inhabitants (a theory pioneered by Modernist painters and sculptors from early-twentieth-century Austria and Germany, who coined the expression *Gesamtkunstwerk*, "complete work of art"). Both of the above examples have huge significance historically, and were extreme and conscious attempts to alter the perception and functionality of the home, but times have changed yet again, and we now have the luxury not to have to resort to such prescriptive tendencies. For centuries up to the 1970s, it was the same with fashion: a clothing style was worn by the masses, then debunked in favor of a more, or sometimes much less, radical approach. We would swing from the bustle to deconstruction, from the miniskirt to the maxi. These days, it seems, anything goes, as long as the attire suits the wearer.

To be elegant, however, the outfit—or the home—must also be appropriate to itself, avoiding contradiction. A simple "insertion" of one interior scheme or period into the shell of another rarely works. For a successful combination, it is vital to find the common threads that run through what you are dealt and what you are attempting to achieve.

With skill and understanding, blends can be spectacular. One of the finest houses to have undergone a recent restoration, a seven-story Federal townhouse in Manhattan, began with five storys and a need for preservation of the original Greek-style embellishments throughout. According to its architects, the New York firm Shelton, Mindel & Associates, it would have been inappropriate to create an old-world Federal interior, since the couple occupying the house are young, dynamic, and lovers of 1930s and '40s French furniture. The house required sensitive restoration, but Mindel wanted to avoid the "insertion" of a more contemporary interior into an older property. The result is a house that begins on basement and ground floors quite classically (the furniture and color schemes—neutral tones, black, and some red—are typical of the early-mid-twentieth-century French, a period that drew on the classics), while the top floors, newly re-created, are starkly modern and light; yet the interior appears seamless throughout, and the essence of the Greek Revival Federalism remains.

CIRCULATION
Successful architecture allows humans to move around with ease; in a building that doesn't work, it is impossible to place furniture properly so that people do not bump into it—and in such circumstances, it is impossible to be stylish. While constriction of movement is the main problem, excessive circulation can also be an issue, an endless succession of doors undermining elegance perhaps as much as bottlenecks and dead ends.

In classical and neoclassical interiors, circulation is a stupendous, symmetrical experience: entrance halls contain sweeping staircases to the left and right, and rooms generally lead off hallways in a logical, mathematical manner—symmetry was meant to unharness the intellect. In America in the eighteenth century, simple Shaker houses also adhered to the

BELOW The main floor of this mid-nineteenth-century house is above ground level, reached via an exquisite staircase whose foot is practically at the front door. This encourages people to go upstairs, a principle in keeping with the original architect's ideas, although the space's axis has been changed, and it has been opened up to allow ease of movement and maximize light.

ABOVE When converting this building from a dilapidated 1920s site into a home, American architect Larry Booth used an extant opening where an industrial skylight had been roofed over to add a staircase. Within the residence, the geometry gives balance and order, and the axes lead you gently from place to place.

BELOW A perfect example of free-flowing space: Andrée Putman completely opened up the rooms of this penthouse, creating through sight-lines. This view from the seafront terrace shows the kitchen corridor with cabinet doors at the end; in front of this, sliding doors on one side lead to the dining niche, which has a view through two sets of windows back toward the terrace.

ABOVE In this Paris duplex apartment, the bedroom can be reached from the living room via a custom-made storage unit with steps at the end. A second pair of sliding doors from the bedroom (not seen here) leads to the bathroom, from which there are more steps back to the living room. Thus the space is fluid, but each "room" has its discrete space.

philosophy of symmetry. They even went so far as to separate men's and women's quarters, giving gender-different circulatory experiences within houses (thus men and women rarely met—in keeping with the sect's philosophy of celibacy).

Bourgeois seventeenth- and eighteenth-century French houses, on the other hand, took the form of strings of rooms leading from one to another, the only departure points being French windows (which are, in fact, doors) or yet another room. The floor plans of such houses, and of the later nineteenth-century Haussmannian apartments, apparently influenced French window treatments: the French open their doors and windows inward, the British and many other Europeans outward. This also relates to the French preference for shutters over curtaining or drapes, which cannot be maneuvered when a window opens in. Some French people say they let the outside beauty in, while the British let the ugliness of their interiors out!

Ironically, one of the most iconic Modernist houses of the twentieth century, a great achievement as an early experiment in completely flowing space—the Villa Savoye, built by Le Corbusier in 1929 at Poissy on the outskirts of Paris—was inspired by the fact that the client's wife was unable to reverse her automobile. The ground floor was therefore designed so the car could be parked under the body of the house, then driven forward to exit in a U-turn, and the curve theme was continued throughout the house. As always, architecture grows out of solving problems. At the Villa Savoye, it is possible to walk from room to room, around all floors, entering and exiting the house—there are terraces on each floor—in a single unidirectional movement, either entering the hallway via the central spiral staircase, then returning by the ramps

LEFT How luxurious to possess not merely a walk-in closet but an entire walk-in room as a closet. The dressing room, once a necessary feature of everyday life in grand houses, has shrunk with the years, partly because our clothes generally do not need as much space as those of our predecessors, nor quite as much care and attention, and we have fewer different garbs for different occasions. But if a dressing room is required, and if the house has ample space, then please do not forget the same principles as for other rooms: give it easy access.

LEFT An ingenious "cabinet" is not what it seems. New Yorker Thad Hayes is a master of technique when it comes to reorganizing existing interior space: the front section of the unit in the hall holds drawers for storage, while the back has become a seating area with a corduroy-covered banquette sofa; thus the back of the "cabinet" contains a room. The two other sides of the cube form walls. The addition of the unit has meant the space has become multipurpose and more fluid. Sometimes adding something can enhance ease of movement.

linking each floor, or vice versa, or a mixture of the two. The house was built for entertaining, and one wonders if this constant circulatory device actually helped or hindered social events; since the body of the house forms a continuous labyrinth, it is possible to be lost for hours.

Good circulation is equally possible, and even more essential, in diminutive spaces. A delightful example is Patrick De Poortere's top-floor apartment on the Belgian coast (*see* pages 38–39), designed by interiors doyenne Andrée Putman in 1999. The original 1960s space was a pathetic hodgepodge of small rooms, although the apartment had a double aspect and sea views. Now it is a completely flowing space, aided by the use of sliding doors and clever niches. The tiny hallway leads to a room that is palatial in feeling, left toward the kitchen, left again into the dining room, and back to the hall. There is a sight-line stretching through from front to back of the apartment, with north and south views visible at once. The hallway also gives access to the bedroom and bath- and shower rooms; the bathroom's two entry points are an inspired contribution to circulation. When I was last there, the six very tall adults wandering around seemed to have ample space to stretch their legs.

For an interior to be elegant, it is also important that the direction of circulation should feel appropriate. An apocryphal tale tells of the legendary American decorator "Sister" Parish, who was responsible for the interior of the White House during President Kennedy's term in office, arriving at a client's newly built home. "It's lovely," she is said to have remarked of the architectural achievement, "but it should be the other way around." We are not told whether the house was rebuilt or "flipped," as Sister Parish had suggested, with the driveway on the left instead of the

right, but the story is illustrative of how some people instinctively know when a space feels right and if circulation within it will be manageable.

My own mother's cottage in England's Berkshire, a preserved building, has a kitchen I find entirely unusable. A very right-handed person, I keep knocking into open cupboards: the kitchen's previous owner was left-handed, and in a very functional room the left-handed/right-handed issue can be a problem. The cottage originally had a larger kitchen with fireplaces, which became a dining room when the current kitchen was added in the 1970s, so perhaps the fundamental problem with Mother's kitchen is that it was an ill-thought-out addition to begin with, its left-handedness just the way the conflict expresses itself.

RIGHT The entrance hall seen through the double doors, with its stone floor design inspired by a floor at Carlos de Beistegui's home at Groussay, is devoid of furniture except for a pair of Biedermeier chairs. The hall leads to an enfilade of bedrooms to one side and the living room on the other. The living room gives access to the library, then a servants' hallway from which a tiny kitchen and service rooms are reached, and finally back to the Chinese-inspired dining room (seen here). The table is from a Chinese restaurant in Paris; its center acts as a "lazy Susan."

LIGHTING

As a medium of design, light is as important as other basic elements—form, color, and texture—and perhaps more so, since it orchestrates our perception of all the other elements. The lighting designer, like an architect, is a problem solver who has to devise the most appropriate arrangement for the job at hand. Like a face awkwardly lit from below, a badly lit room will look ugly, its porportions and tones distorted, whereas good lighting can reapportion space beautifully and to great effect. Light not only allows us to see the full elegance of an interior in detail and to carry out visual tasks, but also affects our attitudes, moods, and behavior. So it is vital that designers and laymen alike weave lighting into the basic design concept. The application of lighting, however, is best left to the professionals—architects and designers, and also lighting engineers, electrical engineers and contractors, building owners and managers, and those supplying fixtures and lamps.

The first steps to creating the right lighting scheme for an interior are assessment of the site and its constraints—which must always be carried out on site

LEFT The joy of Sally Sirkin Lewis's black-and-white interior dining room is the cutout window slits just below the ceiling, which allow daylight gently to bathe the room (she also has an outdoor "room" for dining in the backyard). By night, spotlights create a different mood. The furniture, from Lewis's J. Robert Scott label, includes a glass-topped "Sculpture" table with a polished stainless-steel base. Her own-design dinnerware is accompanied by Venetian Murano glass vases, ebony and sterling-silver Italian flatware, and a grouping of black pebbles.

RIGHT Modern movement architects prided themselves on designing houses that were tailored to the needs of modern living. The indoor/outdoor aspects of many architects' houses built from the 1930s to '60s reflected the importance attached at this time to sunbathing, outdoor exercise, and natural light. Since sunshine was seen as synonymous with health, terraces often took up at least one-third of the living space.

RIGHT Task lighting is a minefield, and just as we now look to chairs of sound ergonomic design for sitting at desks for long periods, we should pay heed to good lighting when carrying out a task. The penetration of daylight can produce better visual contrasts on the task than many of today's lighting systems, but reliance on daylight can raise issues of excessive brightness. A radical imbalance of daylight can be costly: if there is no apparent vertical brightness in the interior, the occupants may turn on indoor lights in an attempt to make indoors as bright as outdoors and correct the perceived darkness.

and after dusk—and analysis of the inhabitants. A lighting concept can then be roughed, tested for feasibility, and refined.

It has long been believed that the most basic factor in ease of seeing is the degree to which detail stands out from the background: larger detail is easier to see, and smaller detail can be made more visible by using more light. Recent research, however, indicates that as the background becomes brighter with more light, the eyes become less sensitive to brightness differences (i.e., contrast), so yet more light is needed. Lights cannot be bright in a field of brightness, only in a field of dimness.

In the mind, brightness is a phenomenon of contrasts, the result of the combined physics of interior finishes and reflected light. Establishing these contrasts is a matter of manipulating finishes as well as lighting, so when considering how to light an

interior, lighting and finishes should be selected simultaneously. Good lighting requires much more than whim, fancy, and artistry; lighting experts have long been able to manipulate visual perception to an enormous extent, and researchers studying the physiology and psychology of seeing are discovering more and more about visual and nonvisual cues that affect perception.

Lighting an interior is about both mood and image. Mood, from the designer's point of view, is more passive, more to do with the visitor's interpretation of the space while experiencing it over a period of time; image is more active, the initial impact created by the lit space on the visitor. Image is of particular concern for the professional designer wishing to comply with a client's perception of how a home should be presented, which in turn is influenced by the activities that are performed in the space. People like to create an impression, even drama, with their interiors, and lighting can give great impact—think of Hitchcock films to appreciate its power.

Significant investigations into the psychology of lighting were carried out in New York in the mid-1970s by John Flynn, Terry Spencer, Osyp Martyniuck, and Clyde Hendrick, who found that different people in different rooms assess lighting in a consistent manner. For instance, if a room is wallwashed with light, both young and older people will experience it as spacious and quiet, and regardless of the room's function, the impression of volume and quietude will persist as long as this light is present. Most people perceive light in exactly the same way. This is not necessarily the case for other interior elements such as color and texture.

One of the great problems with light is metamerism—the phenomenon by which colors change their appearance when viewed in different light conditions. A beige

carpet, for example, will seem completely different in a showroom lit by warm incandescent lighting from its appearance in an office with cool fluorescent lighting. The cooler lighting effectively sucks the life out of a color like beige. Metamerism is almost inevitable with some colors and less problematic with others. Those most likely to be affected are taupe, mauve, lilac, tan, celadon, gray-blues and grays, all of which are favorites in a classic interior. The phenomenon also occurs more subtly in daylight, which changes its effects depending upon the time of day, season,

LEFT Here, a floating wall is lit from behind. True backlighting is a technique whereby light is diffused through translucent materials such as acrylic panels, silk screens, stained glass, marble veneer, and others that have the potential to become luminous. Lighting the back of a floating wall that is not translucent has a completely different effect, making the wall more prominent visually so that it stands as sculpture, as well as lighting the room indirectly. Ceiling spotlights are directed toward family photographs.

RIGHT Spotlights are highlights, and highlighting is a technique that produces more than five times the amount of brightness on a featured object than on the background. The high contrast draws attention. Low-voltage lighting equipment has expanded the usefulness of highlighting immensely: with the very precise optics of low-voltage light bulbs, brightness balances can be created. This technique is often used in museums, where sensitive artifacts benefit from dramatic effects, relying on contrast.

and direction of light (i.e., whether it comes from north or south). The problems of metamerism can be solved by always looking at colors under the kind of light in which they are destined to be seen, but bear in mind that color mutations can also be caused by reflected light from large colored surfaces or mirrors. Metamerism is further complicated by the fact that colors may seem to match, or even be identical, under one light source but look completely different under another—one answer is to use complementary or contrasting colors, so that color match is less of an issue. (In any case, a "match" is often the coward's way out and, let it be said, one of the least elegant of decorating devices.)

The effect of daylight is a hugely complicated field, too. Daylight varies in terms of the depth to which it penetrates an interior, its colors and their compatibility with those of the interior, and the effects of fading. In addition to visible daylight, light from the sun contains wavelengths of invisible light: infrared that dehydrates and cracks some sensitive materials such as wood and rattan; ultraviolet that causes fading on certain pigment colors that are more fugitive or apt to fade.

In some spaces, the penetration of daylight produces better visual contrasts on tasks at hand than do many overhead lighting systems. Therefore, in home offices or areas of activity, deep daylight penetration is a design objective; a higher contrast between printed matter and its background is achieved by daylight entering via side windows instead of skylights.

What happens when daylight fades? Other major issues when planning a lighting scheme include privacy. No one wants their home to look like a goldfish bowl from outside. Nor is it clever to have windows that appear as black mirrors by night, reflecting images of each bright spot in the

LEFT, TOP AND BOTTOM This lamp (top) is throwing light primarily in a downward direction. True downlighting, however, involves directing light at 180 degrees from a fixture aperture on the ceiling. It is used for lighting desk or table tasks, and for ambient lighting in areas with high ceilings, such as double-height rooms. A downlit space normally appears to have light everywhere (brightness only appears on horizontal surfaces; the verticals are lit by indirect or reflected light). Downlighting techniques that designers use specifically for high-ceilinged spaces may not be successful for low-ceilinged rooms, where people may appear ghastly with downlights directly above their heads. People do not benefit from being lit in the same way as furniture. If a designer insists on using downlights in a space with ceilings less than 10 feet (3 meters) high, they must be certain that the user will not be sitting directly beneath the downlight (as, sadly, happens in some restaurants). Objects such as these red glass vases (bottom) and the stylish bathroom (top) do, however, benefit from being lit from overhead.

ABOVE The most subtle of recessed accent ceiling lights. Unlit, these recesses appear to be rectangular, although they are carved with internal angles which direct the light toward the group of artworks beneath. They perform in the same way as spotlights, but to my mind are a much better alternative for their sheer beauty and simplicity of detail.

RIGHT Although a home and its lighting should be planned quite precisely, the odd accident can give a room character. Intentional shadow play, the reverse of beam play, is a technique used by many lighting designers. An interior can be softened by throwing the shadows of plants, for example, on to a wall or a ceiling. Shadows can also be used to expand the scale and impact of three-dimensional forms and sculpture. Here the radiator cover, the plant, and its shadow form their own sculpture.

interior: solutions for correcting these unwanted reflections involve balancing the illumination on both sides of the glass by recessing lights into the outside overhang, where they will brighten vertical surfaces, or directing inside light to strike horizontal surfaces. Of course, by far the easiest method is to have a window covering, such as curtaining or louvered doors.

SPECIALIZED LIGHTING EFFECTS In general, interior lighting follows one of two approaches. In 1912, Dr. Louis Bell laid out the choices in *The Art of Illumination*: "Two courses are open to the designer. In the first place, he can have the whole space lighted uniformly, more or less approximating the effect of a room receiving daylight through its windows. Or, throwing aside any purpose to simulate daylight in intensity or distribution... he can put artificial light simply where it is needed to serve the ends of art and convenience."

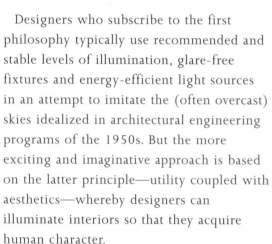

FAR LEFT A sculptural patinated cast-metal lamp throws light onto a resin table. Matte surfaces absorb light, and then refract it, thus softening it. So if, for example, porcelain vases are mounted against a matte rich-red wall, the matte red encourages the ambient light to bury itself in the wall, and by contrast, the cool gloss of the white porcelain reflects its luster. The combination of an absorbent surface behind a reflective one projects the vases forward visually.

LEFT In Swedish designer Martin Brudnizki's *pied-à-terre*, wall lights throw light upward in the bed area (a technique used in restaurants to provide soft illumination and add romance). A large cube lamp shade throws light down onto the table and also diffuses it through the room via its satin-covered body.

LEFT Recessed ceiling lights throw beams onto copper-mesh cupboard doors. Although it is an industrial material, the copper creates effective play of light. Illuminated cabinets around the sink unit, from which diffused light emits through frosted glass, help light the room and give a futuristic feel. "Light is infinitely varied when brought into contact with different materials," says designer Andrée Putman.

Designers who subscribe to the first philosophy typically use recommended and stable levels of illumination, glare-free fixtures and energy-efficient light sources in an attempt to imitate the (often overcast) skies idealized in architectural engineering programs of the 1950s. But the more exciting and imaginative approach is based on the latter principle—utility coupled with aesthetics—whereby designers can illuminate interiors so that they acquire human character.

Within this second approach, there are many forms of lighting to suit different purposes. Wallwashing is a technique whereby a wall is unified with a sheet of bright light, which produces various effects: the space is given directionality, in that people who enter the room are drawn across it toward that wall; diverse objects placed on the wall are linked together because they and the space between them are seen, literally, in the same light; the texture of the wall seems flattened; and substantial quantities of gentle light are bounced back into the space.

ABOVE Another elegant material for lamps is cast bronze, patinated or polished—a passion of the early-twentieth-century Paris set, who used it for standing lamps, often adorned with leaves or figures. Plaster was also favored for lights by many artists and artisans associated with Paris in the 1930s and '40s, including Jean-Michel Frank, Christian Bérard, and Alberto and Diego Giacometti, who took sea-shell and spiral forms as a prime inspiration.

Highlighting, or accent lighting, picks out specific objects and surfaces in an otherwise darker environment, focusing people's attention and thereby influencing how they sit and move in a space. The entire space can be composed into a unified whole by highlighting. An extension of this technique is beam play, by which perhaps a hallway or corridor is highlighted.

Shadow play is the reverse of beam play, and involves the negative space. Here the pattern of light is the background; the shape of the shadow carries the visual message. Silhouetting, on the other hand, is a technique that sandwiches an object between the viewer and a beam of light: the object is outlined by light, whose brightness acts as negative space.

Apart from structural lighting (which is a method of mounting fixtures such as moldings to conceal backlighting), other lighting techniques for the home include downlighting (usually used for distributing ambient light throughout spaces with high ceilings so there are no distracting bright lights) and uplighting (which creates upwardly lit movable pools of ambient light, usually by way of floor lamps—although uplighting can include the use of uniformly spaced suspended lights that light a space entirely indirectly). Then there is grazing, a technique whereby a grazing angle of light causes the texture of the vertical surface to sneak into view: to create a grazing relationship between a textured surface and rays of light, downlights are used 6 to 12 inches (15 to 30 centimeters) away from the vertical surface to be grazed, resulting in a staccato pattern of brightness and shadow.

Generally speaking, decisions on which of the above to use are determined by the activities to be undertaken in each room. The appropriate amount of light for an activity is affected by several factors: the color of light, the angle of light, and the spatial distribution in both the immediate environment and the distant view field. Task lighting, which is the level of light needed for the eyes and brain to perform a task, can be achieved by either uniform ambient lighting or specific task lighting—and it is a good idea to take into consideration the quality of vision of the people who will be active in that space.

Non-task lighting is a fascinating issue, and rooms intended for through movement or repose rather than specific tasks are fraught with subtle variables. Lighting not only affects our moods, but also influences our behavior in subconscious ways. So by using light and color to manage the cues we unknowingly perceive, the homemaker or designer also manages behavior.

When a person enters a space, they automatically scan it (generally from left to right), first reading any faces present, followed by the relationship of planes and surfaces. It is this relationship between the brightnesses of surfaces that gives people visual cues about how to use a space. The human response to brightness cues has been confirmed by studies published in 1973 by the Illuminating Engineering Society, which conclude that, unconsciously, our minds and bodies seek out and are drawn to light: people are phototropic. This is one of the most powerful influences on lighting in designed spaces, applied through techniques such as accent lighting and wallwashing. In a non-task room or a traffic room (where people move around more than in other rooms), colors of the highest reflectivity should be used, and higher light levels should be focused on the surfaces toward which the occupants should focus and move. This will encourage smooth circulation and, on a subconscious level, will just feel right—essential ingredients for a classic interior.

SHAPE

There is no blueprint for shape in a classic interior, nor are there particular types of shapes that are inherently more elegant. The key requisite is cadence—a balanced and harmonious relationship between the various elements.

Balance does not mean uniformity. There is a misconception that, for instance, a successfully sleek, minimalist "modern" room must contain only contemporary, vertical and rectilinear furniture and objects. But in fact, a room will benefit more from carefully thought-out variety in shapes and ages. Consider the Georgian and Regency periods, when lines were generally straight, yet elegant bowed furniture was placed according to its visual effect on the entire space. In chic modern room settings incorporating furniture and decorative objects, the contemporary lump must be

leavened by traditional elements that give shape, form, and accent. Taken straight, the starkness and boldness of contemporary design (think of Philippe Starck's furniture) without older, less mathematical accents can be too inhospitable, institutional, and undistinguished to live with. It needs to be broken up with friendlier elements, beautiful objects from a variety of past periods with a variety of texture and form, mellowing and modifying the present and ubiquitous straight line. This is evident in the Zucker residence in Chicago (*see* pages 36–37), where the emphatic restrictions are mellowed by a vast floor-to-ceiling pitted-metal fire surround—a humanizing device in a strict architectural shell.

An interior is like a still life, a satisfying arrangement of objects. Order and the relationships between objects, their shape

and scale, must be considered in relation to the microcosm—such as a few tiny items or pebbles arranged in a bowl—as much as the macrocosm of the entire room. The same applies to fashion: the choice of whether to wear pearl earrings is just as important as the choice of the little black dress; their spherical form might just as easily accent as detract from the entire look. In clothing, art, or interiors, the elimination of any element, because of its shape and scale in relation to other objects, can destabilize the whole sense of order and form. Of course, it is relatively easy for the artist to change something that doesn't suit, whereas the designer or decorator has to unearth a suitable alternative, unless the entire interior and contents are custom-designed—which in my opinion can lead to too much order, eluding the random poetry of the incidental *objet trouvé* that is just ever-so-slightly off-beam.

It is possible to have too much order. With the advent of Surrealism around the time of World War I, Salvador Dali, Henri Matisse, and other painters sought to realize the philosophy that only subconscious "unreason" could yield true art. The stylish interior could be argued to be similar: only the workings of the subconscious should be evident. An imperfect cadence can prove a more sophisticated, satisfactory, and unpredictable conclusion to a symphony of form than a perfect one.

The stimulus of unreason and cross-fertilization of disciplines continued through the twentieth century. After World War I, Modernism triggered intellectual expansion in all the arts: artists painted in an architectural manner; architects built in a painterly way (Le Corbusier was a painter before becoming an architect). There was Constructivism in Russia, Cubism in France, and De Stijl in Holland, and a fragmentation of form toward abstraction. The radical work of Picasso and Braque around 1910 was part of a transformation in the world at large. In science, atomic theories of matter and new concepts of space, time, and energy were challenging long-accepted theories: Einstein's Special Theory of Relativity (1905) had shown that measurements at any given moment were not fixed, but varied depending upon the relative position and movement of the viewer. These attitudes gained currency in the 1920s, translated through to painting, and remain the blueprint for our perception of form, shape, and relative position. Like Picasso and Braque, we enjoy exploring the tension between abstraction and practical reality, and in opposing the two we strive for a fine balance. In creating interiors with an eye to shape, form, and relativity, we are participating in a kind of abstraction of art.

Architects' contributions to furniture design owe much to their understanding of shape and form. The Viennese-born R. M. Schindler (1887–1953), who set up a practice in Los Angeles in 1921, designed for his own projects furniture influenced by the Arts and Crafts movement, Art Nouveau, and Viennese Secession of his student days. In the 1950s, Eero Saarinen and Charles Eames of Michigan's Cranbrook Academy, two of the great Modernist designers, discussed chairs in terms of "architecture in miniature." Their chairs, like those created by Ludwig Mies van der Rohe for the Barcelona Exhibition of 1929, were designed to stand away from the wall, to be viewed from all angles as if sculpture, and, with sound ergonomics, to support the sitter in comfort, fusing art and technology.

LEFT Sally Sirkin Lewis helped revive the popularity of Lucite as a material for furniture half a century after it came into being. Completely transparent, it lends itself to simple curved forms. The geometric nature of some of Lewis's products, even her French-made tapestry cushions, adds to the room's visual content, with its dramatic geometric art and curvilinear metal sculpture.

RIGHT The straight, angular lines of the cabinet and artwork could not be stricter. Offsetting them are a porcelain relief—a limited edition by Victor Pasmore for Rosenthal, circa 1972—and a "melted" time-piece sculpture, a Salvador Dali edition. The late 1930s parchment-fronted Italian cabinet in various woods has "winged victory" feet and a fine mirrored interior.

ABOVE FAR RIGHT The curvature of a bay window overlooking Chicago's Lake Michigan is exquisitely enhanced by the line of the "Racine" table in ropework by French designer Christian Astuguevieille, its legs reminiscent of elephant trunks. The carved chair by Rose Tarlo is almost Gaudí-esque in form, its rawness complementing an otherwise genteel setting.

RIGHT "Proportion is the first principle, and proper appropriation of the parts constitutes symmetry and harmony," said architectural commentator Robert Morris in 1751. Here, in New York, perfect neoclassical symmetry is offset by the natural shape of the shell underneath the table. The path of classical influence over the centuries and up to the present day highlights its enduring strength.

SYMMETRY

"The first reality that rules a room is the space that determines its size.... The second reality is the function for which the room has been planned. The third is the decoration that, in harmony with the architecture, will be able to correct its defects, apportion its effects, and create illusions." So said the late Milan architect Renzo Mongiardino, a consummate creator of spectacular, atmospheric spaces. In his "roomscapes," life branched out according to the scheme of the Italian palazzo, and symmetry—of architecture, decoration, and furnishing—was fundamental to elegance.

The early-sixteenth-century Italian architect Andrea Palladio was one of the first to influence Western architecture toward perfect symmetry and equilibrium. The principal influence on his work was classical antiquity, studied at first hand in Rome. His early style was similar to that of the High Renaissance architect Donato d'Agnolo Bramante (1444–1514); later he was influenced by Michelangelo and contemporary Mannerism. At Vicenza in northern Italy, Palladio built the so-called Basilica in 1549, along with many palaces and the Teatro Olimpico, modeled on classical theaters. His best-known work was the Villa Rotonda or Capra, built circa 1550 near Vicenza, one of many summer houses designed also to be farms. The villa's entrance portico is repeated on all four sides; this symmetry combined with simple mathematical proportions is the main feature of his work. On a smaller scale, the Palladian window or motif (introduced by Serlio but popularized by Palladio) consists of a central arched opening flanked by a smaller rectangular opening on each side. Columns usually separate the openings.

Palladio's treatise *I Quattro Libri dell'Architettura*, published in 1570, was translated into numerous languages and had a lasting influence on architecture internationally. Palladian architecture, characterized by symmetry, monumentality, and academic use of classical forms, is found not only in Italy: the term is also applied to eighteenth-century architecture in England, where taste relied heavily on the designs of Palladio and of Inigo Jones (1537–1651), who introduced High Renaissance architecture into Britain. Many an English country house boasts a Palladian villa's combination of grandeur, agricultural utility, and porticoes.

In any period, symmetry, in furniture and architecture, is fundamental in re-creating the balance and monumentality of ancient Rome and Greece. Georgian, Federal, Regency, French Empire, Directoire—in all these, lines are sleek, proportions perfect. Two-dimensional symmetry is not enough; well-balanced complex combinations and perfect curves assure greater success.

For such interiors, compass-drawn curves are better than ellipses, while flat-topped "arches" seem arches more by definition than appearance, like flat feet compared with the lofty airiness of a compass-drawn curve. However, any arches provide a good combination of room divider and look-through. Arches in series—witness the rue de Rivoli in Paris or Roman aqueducts—are lighter, more graceful, and more vertical in feeling than a single arch can ever be.

Multiple geometry is not only elegant but also steadying; a single Directoire chair almost always benefits from a partner. The Directoire era in late-eighteenth-century France was influenced by both Louis XVI and French Empire styles, and by the politics of France's Directorate, a time of studied and ingenious simplification and reform. The fine French hand devoted itself to line, without ornamental distractions, and achieved a classicism of its own. What little ornament there was was understated: all followed the plainest of

RIGHT Two sofas back to back create symmetry on two axes. Suzani fabric in unusually muted colors (it is more often found in brighter reds and blues) covers the pillow on the sofa. A circular marble-topped French Empire table and a pair of nineteenth-century Baltic *klismos* chairs create a classical scene, although the overall effect is very contemporary indeed. As Jacob von Falke wrote in 1873, "In so far as style is concerned, the modern Frenchman dwells in the eighteenth century, he sleeps in that century likewise, but he dines in the sixteenth... smokes his cigar and enjoys his coffee in the Orient, while he takes his bath in Pompeii, in Ancient Greece." In essence, the classical vocabulary of decoration may demand balance, but it also allows great variety.

FAR RIGHT Asymmetry can be harmonious if the proportions are as considered as in a symmetrically designed room. Here, the "boxing" of the wall provides a framework within which the four elements— the two pieces of art, the chair and the lectern—are contained. The 1930s-style chairs (one seen here) are the modern work of Canadian furniture designer Thomas Lamb.

geometry, the mechanically drawn straight line, the purest of symmetry.

The splendor of French Empire style also appealed to the British, who, during the English Regency, adopted it all but intact. Along with an enthusiasm for Greek and Egyptian shapes and objects, Rome passed on Doric and Ionic architecture as standard components of furniture and architectural design. *Klismos* chairs, rosewood and black lacquer, marble and bronze busts and statues of classical heroes appeared at every turn. (A less demure Regency was evident from time to time, as in the Brighton Pavilion, but mainly it was simple, severe, masculine, and elegant.) Similar fashions were popular at the time not only in France, but in Germany (Biedermeier) and the United States (Duncan Phyfe), too.

Any combination of these tasteful styles, their ancestors or offspring, can sit well together, as long as objects are placed in pairs or symmetrical multiples, as originally intended. Symmetrical bodies and balanced minds belong in a room that displays a measure of symmetry and order.

RIGHT French Empire and Directoire chairs derive much of their elegance from their fine, curving symmetry. Many types of seating found in today's classical-style interiors were, in fact, developed long after the decline of the Roman Empire. Chairs with upholstered seats first appeared in the late sixteenth century; prior to this, loose squab cushions were used. However, in terms of both basic form and decorative embellishment, many chairs, including Directoire and French Empire styles, owe a great deal to the wooden, bronze, and marble prototypes made in ancient Greece and Rome.

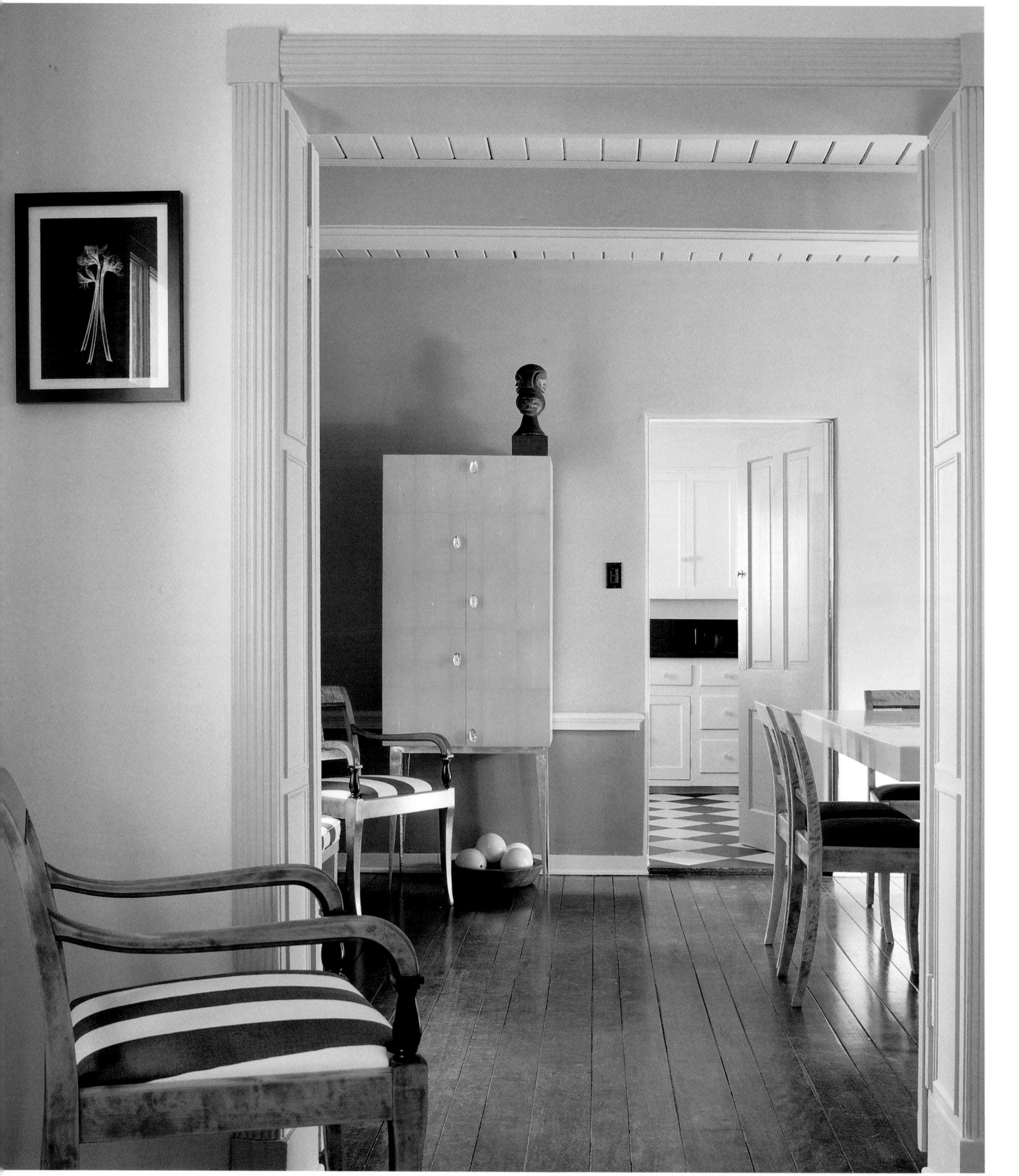

COLOR

Color is the first thing you are aware of in a room: it takes precedence over period, design, arrangement, and quality. It is one of the potentially most rewarding ingredients of an interior, and can also be one of the least expensive to apply, at any rate in the case of plastered walls. On the down side, it can be the most complicated to deal with, next to lighting, and if insensitively handled, color can effectively destroy a room of beautiful natural proportions.

The most plastic of all design elements, color is also the most chameleonlike. Perhaps only potters delight in color mutations: the very act of submitting their wares to a trial by fire is surely a surrender of complete control. For the rest of us, there is nothing more frustrating than a false or varying perception of color, as highlighted by Josef Albers in his color-theory classes at Yale University. Albers asked thirty students to paint the most intense red imaginable. No two reds were the same—some were pinkish, others more brown. He also observed that Coca-Cola produced two kinds of red for their bottle-tops: a cool red for the south and a warm red for the north.

The principles of color, both in scientific terms and decoration-wise, and the effects of lighting, should be understood before embarking upon any choice of color for the home. For instance, in dim lighting the human eye can see the violet/blue end of the spectrum better than reds. Because of this shift (called the Purkinje effect after the researcher who discovered it), in dim light reds often appear gray, while blues take on an ethereal brightness. This begs questions: did Renaissance artists consciously paint blues in churches for this effect? Is the Virgin Mary so often shown attired in blue because the color remains unaltered in dimly lit chapels?

Most designers refer to the use of color in an interior as a "scheme," which in my opinion can be a little misleading in reference to color, since it conjures up a place perhaps too evenly considered, too neat in its entirety, and thus unimaginative. It sounds as if the color "scheme" exists in isolation, which it does not: it remains part of the unified whole of an interiors scheme (better usage). I prefer to talk in terms of color enhancement, accent or background colors, but in deference to other writers and experts on the subject, and for lack of a suitable alternative term, will refer to "schemes" when attempting to clarify the basic considerations relating to color and color theory.

Color schemes fall into three general groups: monochromatic, related, and contrasting. In theory, a monochromatic scheme features a single color in a variety of shades and textures; in practice, in the "chicest" of interiors, minor accents or pinpricks of contrast tend to emphasize its monochromatic nature. Interiors adhering to these color principles can be very stylish indeed. A related scheme is one of bountiful color, using colors that lie close together on the rainbow spectrum (e.g., a series of reds and oranges, or greens and blues). This is a system not entirely typical of classic interiors, unless it is very sensitively applied. Perhaps the most sophisticated is a scheme of contrasting colors, in which the colors or their weights are widely different, and there are many subtleties to consider.

Devising a color scheme for a home can be a daunting task. It is imperative first to think about the whole before planning any individual areas, and to work out a storyboard and sketches of how a space or collection of rooms will come together. Analyze each room in terms of function, and select a series of color schemes that will relate well to one another—examine the meeting points of different wall and floor finishes, and make sure that they are either harmonious or contrasting in terms of color, texture, and pattern. Consider the various views from one room to another and select colors that, by eye, coordinate successfully.

PALETTES

PALETTES The human eye can see seven million colors. Most of them are eyesores, and certain color relationships can be irritants, cause headaches, and wreak havoc with our vision. Consequently, the appropriate choice of color can not only bring beauty to a home, but maximize productivity (if needed), minimize visual fatigue, or relax the entire body.

Almost any color can contribute to an interior, and monochromatic schemes can be just as exciting as those using related or contrasting colors—but in all cases, the approach must be wholehearted and bold. However, the marketing mantra "today's sensation is tomorrow's blank stare" sums up the ebb and flow of color trends, and elegance rarely follows fad. Many proponents of the chic interiors of today, the classics of the future, favor muted neutral or monochromatic tones as a base for tranquility and sometimes fine art. A neutral color scheme is flexible and easy to update, revive, or accent. Background neutrals help to create the feeling of order and moods appropriate to classic chic.

This said, a more colorful interior is not necessarily a temporary or inelegant one, and designers and home owners who mix pigments enthusiastically until they produce their desired wash of color (*see* the Paris apartment of decorator Nye Basham, pages 28–29 and 81) are usually very content with the results of their labors. With an element of forethought, these color schemes tend not to date.

Visualize the versatility of a pale greenish-gray drawing room, reminiscent of the grandeurs of St. Petersburg in Russia when a touch of gold leaf is added; the delicacy of a pale rose pink in a boudoir; the luxuriousness of chocolate brown in a dressing room; or Swedish blue in an elegant dining room. Dark hues—blackish green, indigo—can be equally stylish, on one or more walls of a room.

Some shades are valued for their historical significance. Due to its prohibitive cost, the color known as

LEFT, TOP Natural hues and materials do not always have to look rustic, and many wood tones together can make an interesting ensemble. Woods no longer have to be dark-stained and highly polished to be elegant: paler woods and unusual graining have been popular for interiors since the 1940s and are becoming classics. The chic rug is of woven leather strips.

Theoretically, a monochromatic color scheme features a single color in a variety of shades and textures, but in reality this is difficult to achieve. It is possible, however, to create a monochromatic-looking scheme in which a combination of, for instance, grays and "greige" (a cross between gray and beige) is the starting point. Here, the walls are cement plaster with steel wainscoting; the low table is of ancient cedar found in a lumberyard, the antique wooden stool African.

LEFT, BOTTOM When a single color is used in a room, different impressions of depth of color automatically come into play. These are dependent upon the textures used, since light alters the perception of color as it strikes different textures and surfaces. Ideally, lighting and finishes should be selected at the same time.

royal or Tyrian purple, made by draining the glandular mucus of snails, for centuries symbolized extreme wealth and grandeur— Cleopatra's barge was purple, and in Imperial Rome, only the Emperor wore the color. Then in 1856, the chemist William Perkin accidentally changed the face of dyeing with a treatment of coal tar that produced mauve; but purples and mauves

remain unusual wall colors, and it requires confidence to live alongside them.

When choosing color palettes, there are four specifics to consider: hues of colors, their chroma level or intensity, their light reflectance value (*see* page 82), and the contrasts between them. Small variations can radically change the way colors look together and their subconscious impact.

LEFT Jackie Villevoye has created her own bold art wall with a triptych, each panel a different (but related) matte "color." Interestingly, to the left of the artwork, the wall is painted a slightly different "white" from the section of the same wall to its right. The variation is hardly discernible in daylight, since the left is toward the window wall and therefore sunnier. However, at night and with clever lighting, this subtle device makes the artwork stand out more because of the contrast. The unusual approach is feasible only because the art stretches from floor to ceiling.

RIGHT A related scheme makes use of a few or many colors from one part of the color spectrum. In a scheme that will endure, it is far more interesting to use many greens and blues than just one of each. The owners of this apartment in London have chosen blues, greens, and purples for the dining room, which houses, among other things, collections of Han-dynasty Chinese horses and pots, their terracotta color brought alive by the choice of blue/green palette. Each of the three rooms seen here is painted a different shade of putty—again, the variation is hardly discernible, but is effective as a backdrop for the subtle changes in each room.

The basic science of color is frequently misunderstood. If you mix together any two of the primary colors (red, yellow, and blue—the three colors that cannot be created from other colors), you will make secondary colors, namely orange, green, and purple. These six colors are traditionally presented on a color wheel in their natural order to explain the relationship between colors and how new ones are created (this is not a modern concept—it was Sir Isaac Newton who first developed a circular diagram of colors in 1666). Tertiary colors are formed by

contrast can mean maximum stability. "Analogous" colors are any three colors that lie side-by-side on a twelve-part color wheel, such as yellow-green, yellow, and yellow-orange.

Developing a sophisticated sense of color can come only through experiment and an understanding of how color works. It is difficult, for example, to imagine a combination of tertiary colors in the mind's eye—to put complicated color blends together takes skill and time, more than imagination. An old adage suggests we should look to flora and fauna as

FAR RIGHT Related ocher-based hues can be extremely effective when a lot of color is needed to bring life into a room. I like to see strange ocher colors on walls in rooms with northerly light (in the northern hemisphere, that is; southerly light in the southern). The Swedes, in contrast, favor blues and grays, which can be cold in the northern light but nevertheless ethereal in their beauty. Here, the simple addition of pillows and a headboard in related tones brings extra life into a crisp, predominantly white room.

mixing secondary colors, and appear as yellow-orange, red-orange, red-purple, blue-purple, blue-green, and yellow-green. When white is added to a color or hue, it is known as a tint. The addition of black to a color or hue creates a shade. A lightened orange is therefore not a shade of orange, but a tinted orange. Tone refers to the degree of brightness.

Colors directly opposite one another on the wheel are termed complementary: when the eye sees one, it naturally craves the balance of the other, and maximum

inspiration, although I believe we can find inspiration in many quarters, including the study of great painters of yesteryear, from Titian to Francis Bacon.

To adopt a color palette for a room where, say, four neutrals, including beige and taupe, sit comfortably with ocher-based greens and magenta, or for a room where the mystery of dark burl-wood tones and black and white is augmented with cochineal red alongside burnt orange, is anathema to most. According to the textbooks, these hues are not meant to live

BELOW An indigo wall, brown upholstery, "orange" in the wood of the table, and the red of the flowers make a sumptuous conglomeration of color. The moodiness of this room has been pushed to the limits by this bold statement. Always paint a substantial section of a wall to sample paint colors, and try and try again if you are not wholly satisfied that you are making the right choice. A paint swatch can never be enough to go by. And be warned: colors always appear darker when applied to larger areas—although this may be the desired effect, of course.

together. The stunning results that they can bring, if wisely applied, depends not only upon the colors themselves and the weight of color, but on the proportion of one color to another. An elegant woman might be fond of color and add a celadon-green headscarf or hat to a black, brown, and red ensemble, but would not attempt to wear all four colors in equal quantity for fear of looking like a harlequin. It is the same with the home.

If a color scheme works, it will exhibit harmony and a sense of dynamic equilibrium. In visual experiences, harmony is something pleasing to the eye that engages the viewer and creates an inner sense of order, a balance in the visual experience. Where harmony does not exist, the effect is either uninteresting—a visual experience so bland that the viewer is not engaged—or, if the human brain is not capable of interpreting what it sees, chaotic. Color harmony delivers visual interest and at the same time a sense of logical order, stimulating our brains neither too little nor too much.

ABOVE A contrasting scheme is one in which the colors used are from different parts of the spectrum, in some cases from extremes, as in the living room of art specialist Maureen Paley's ex-workman's cottage in London. Most difficult to achieve, but highly effective if successful, is a contrasting scheme using different weights of color. Paley waited twenty years before finally deciding which red to use to upholster her sofa (it is officially "Venetian" red, I have been told). The turquoise fringe boosts the singularity of choice. Pale duck's-egg walls are in sharp contrast to the wallpaper. The wooden table is by Jérôme Abel Seguin; the cake is art.

In classic interiors, if a ceiling is to be white, a tiny amount of
the wall color (if pale blue, gray, or green) should be mixed
in, to make it look whiter. Traditionally, molding is true white.
Nye Basham was so careful about his salon color that he
changed his mind by a fraction as the paint dried. The eventual
grayish green is perfect—neither celadon nor "institutional"
green, but a very pretty color that contrasts with the coral and
brown pillows and the true gray of the upholstery.

BACKGROUND COLORS AND LIGHT REFLECTANCE

Background sets the tone. Light-colored floors or walls continuing through a series of rooms can create a sense of space and unity; a dark floor anchors a room. Reds and oranges advance toward you visually, while blues and greens appear to recede and feel spacious.

To work well, background colors must be used in a balanced way. White can provide the perfect background for a range of other colors, but becomes sterile and isolating if used indiscriminately without adequate relief. Black, the most dramatic color, must be treated with caution in the home, unless applied in small quantities alongside other colors. Only the very brave attempt black rooms, but these can be highly chic. Gray is neither hot nor cold, a neutral often considered negative in effect, yet it provides enormous support to other hues. All browns are grounding and supportive—brown is widely considered the color of commitment and stability. Due to its earthiness, it can backdrop almost any other hue.

Background colors also need appropriate lighting. Lighter hues are naturally more reflective than darker ones, and if a scheme contains both light and dark, the lighter colors will be better suited to relatively reflective finishes. Dark walls, in contrast, reflect less: far more lighting is necessary in rooms with dark walls than in those with light ones. In addition, particularly in rooms with dark walls, it is a good idea to make sure that ceilings are light and reflective.

Paint manufacturers can tell you the light reflectance value (LRV) of any color of paint (white, for example, reflects 80 percent of light, black only 5 percent—so the ratio between white and black is 16:1). The higher the LRV, the less artificial light you will need. (According to the Environmental Protection Agency, electric lighting accounts for 25 percent of all electricity used in the United States.) But an extremely high lighting level combined with very light walls can create glare and excessive brightness, which can cause eye irritability and overstimulation. On the other hand, too much contrast is not helpful either: the Illuminating Engineering Society of North America recommends a maximum LRV ratio of 3:1 between a visual task and its background.

The color of a room also affects our perception of its temperature. Tests have shown that people estimate the temperature of a room with "cool" colors, such as blues and greens, to be 6–10 degrees Fahrenheit (3–5.5 degrees Centigrade) cooler than its actual temperature. "Warm" reds and oranges result in estimates 6–10 degrees Fahrenheit warmer. Color therefore plays an important role in energy conservation: a "warm"-colored room's actual temperature can be kept significantly cooler than that of a similar but "cool"-colored room.

The choice of background color can, it seems, affect not only utility bills, but also well-being and mood, according to color therapists, who study the healing vibrations of different colors.

Red, for example—the final brush of lipstick on a classic interior—raises the blood pressure and quickens the heartbeat, and can rouse us to activity, which may be why it tends to appeal to younger people. Orange and yellow are linked to the intellect, and although they radiate different "energies," they both have the ability to raise spirits (orange can actually stimulate the appetite and aid digestion, which is why it is considered appropriate for kitchens and dining rooms). When viewed next to the neutrality of gray, the vibrancy of orange is accentuated (so if

OPPOSITE If backgrounds in a classic interior are to be colored rather than neutral, their colors should ideally be taken from the part of the spectrum comprising greens, blues, and mauves; the range from lime green through yellow and orange to red is generally best kept for accent color only. This approach holds true whether the interior is neoclassical or modernist, whether sophisticated or relatively simple. Pale blues and greens (top and bottom left) can be calming: like the sky, blue is infinite and heavenly, cooling and pacifying. Green has obvious associations with nature and is especially good for urban areas where there is little access to parks or the countryside. It, too, is comforting and stress-relieving. Used near windows, it can serve to introduce the greens of nature into a room. The atmosphere of all these colors is easily changed according to what is placed with them—a gray chair brings out the blue of a pale hue, just as gray eyeshadow brings out the blue of eyes. The warmth of wooden furniture (top right) accentuates the richness of darker blues and greens, echoing the colors of nature without losing sophistication; even a hint of gold molding feels natural in such a scheme. Walls (and ceilings and floors) that are glossy or very pale will inter-reflect light between them, and thus require much less lighting than dark matte walls. Within a room, the resulting contrast can effectively direct the eye, as well as people's movement. Purple is a contemplative color, and a purple room, or even a single purple wall (bottom right), creates a dignified space for retreat. It should not be a choice for the most active of rooms, such as kitchens, because it can discourage heavy physical work. It is fine in a study, however, because of its ability to bring out the intuitive side of your nature (it is also good for you if you are feeling helpless or ill).

FAR LEFT Green is a good accent color as well as a good background. It is the only color the eye needs no adjustment to see, and can thus be very soothing to look at. Lime hues, however, contain more yellow than blue pigment, making them much more active, alert, and lively. Too much yellow in lime feels unsettling to many people.

LEFT The gray chair acts as neutral support here to a bright coral color. Quiet shades of gray are best used in a supporting role, although they can also be a feature in their own right. The gold of the screen behind is a good choice: gold is often easier to employ alongside hot colors, such as reds and oranges, while silver is better when associated with blues and violets.

ABOVE Red is a color of primal energy and passion. But too much red can lead to nervous tension and aggression, and induce overactivity, so it must be chosen carefully—for the right rooms and in the right proportion. Here it is an energizing force: although used in some quantity, it is repeated on a suite of furniture and helps form the tenet of the room. Imagine if the chairs and settee were covered in muted green. We would probably fall asleep.

BELOW The red of a Gerrit Rietveld "Utrecht" chair, with its divine blanket stitch at every seam, seems brighter still when placed against the black of the carpet. Here the statement is relatively extreme: although red is *the* accent color for a truly stylish interior, it sometimes suffices to add just a dash of the color by way of a pillow. A particular favorite of its owners, this chair deserves its pride of place in an otherwise black-and-white room.

orange is used as a background, it is better to combine it not with gray but with other subtle colors).

Green—created by mixing cool and warm colors—is associated with balance and harmony, and relieves stress. It is ideal for rooms of repose, or where decisions are made, since its supportive nature is not conducive to argument (by all accounts, green also helps to balance the flow of blood, which is one reason, historically, why surgeons wear green).

Azure blues can be helpful in opening up the confines of less spacious rooms. Blue is linked to the body's immunity and can be restorative in bath- or shower rooms: it helps slow the heartbeat and lowers blood pressure, relaxing both muscles and mind. With blue comes serenity: a sound sleeper will find a calm night of rest in a dark blue room, but the sluggish might find it difficult rising in the morning, so be warned if your temperament is such (there is good reason for melancholy songs being called "the blues").

Violet is a color of dignity and respect, and is associated with a meditative environment, yet it can also feel fast and light. It is elegant when combined with wood (which gives it grounding) and is considered the most sophisticated of colors. It is said this color often accompanies times of spiritual growth, and in some cultures it is associated with the passing from life to death.

ACCENT COLORS Highlighting with color can be dramatic, whether simply in the form of a colored glass vase against a dark table lit by a lamp, or as a painting on the wall (*see* Holly Hunt, pages 30–31). Blue glass provides a magical color when illuminated, and blue vases, glasses, and door and wall panels create short bursts of intense blue "energy." Colored glass is so

effective that color therapists employ it for concentrating rays during treatment.

In addition to basic definitions of color and harmony, the manner in which color behaves in relation to other colors, and to shape—"color context"—is a complex area of color theory. Red, for example, is a popular accent color in the classic interior, particularly because it behaves well against neutrals. But beware: the same shade of red will appear more brilliant against a black background and significantly duller against white (red also appears larger against black than against other backgrounds). When contrasted against orange, red appears lifeless; with blue-green it exhibits utter brilliance. True indigo, meanwhile, is such a dark color that it is best used only in accent against neutrals: if over-used, it can be oppressive and subduing.

The neutrality and tranquility of gray as a background exert a steadying influence upon very defined colors such as purple and indigo when these are used as accent colors. Grays are most effective when serving to steady more vibrant colors that, without neutral support, may be too uncontained (all colors benefit from the presence of gray, depending upon the extent to which they are used). When gray is lacking, so are structure, sustenance, and support—imagine a world without the occasional gray sky or expanse of concrete (one of my favorite building materials, when handled by the likes of architects such as the Japanese Tadao Ando). However, if gray is allowed to predominate completely, without accent, it becomes the color of the uncommitted.

Observing the effects colors have on each other is the starting point for understanding the relativity of color. The best way to achieve accent color in the home is by trial and error.

TEXTURE

Texture may be much less obvious to the eye than color, but it, too, is integral to any interior, and particulary important in a classic scheme, where subtlety is vital. A room's collage, its depth and contrast, is augmented by the use of combinations of texture on walls and floors, as well as in the minutiae. While color is essentially a pleasure for the eyes (although it is generally observed that sight-impaired people sense heat and vibration from color, too), texture, and the use of differing textures, not only develops an interior scheme so that it becomes more multifaceted, but also widens its appeal to senses other than sight. Furthermore, like lighting and color, texture can affect behavior, and in temperate climates the altering or addition of textures can be invaluable in changing a typical summery room into a cozy wintery cocoon.

There are some artful designers who manage to create a room to suit all seasons by regarding the whole room as a composite of textures that require balance against an equally textured backdrop (the use of color here demands enormous thought to achieve the right balance). The resulting rooms display a chameleon quality without in principle changing their base color or texture. The simple addition of velvet cushions, say, to warm a north-facing room (in the northern hemisphere), or jute cushions to add cool comfort to a warm sunroom, is a time- and money-saving device which, in its simplicity, is classic in essence. It is like the addition of a short-sleeved cashmere sweater to any attire—a look standardized by some of the most stylish women in modern history, from Princess Grace of Monaco to Björk—whether thrown over a pair of slacks or an evening gown. In similarly classic style, a penthouse apartment designed by Andrée Putman (*see* pages 38–39) in Knokke-Le-

Zoute in Belgium has grayish teak-lined walls that give a librarylike coziness in winter, yet in summer take on an almost beach-hut persona.

Many people, however, whether living a grand or demure lifestyle, choose to change fabrics seasonally. For example, chenille, mohair-velvet, or cashmere curtains can be replaced by unlined cotton, silk, calico, or muslin in the summer months, and cotton or linen slipcovers added to heavier wool-upholstered seating. All of this can be very appealing, provided the bones of the interior accept such change visually.

If the chameleon effect is not for you, it is perfectly possible to create a commodious interior suited to all weathers by using textures equipped to deal with any eventuality. Leather, for instance, is highly popular as a chair covering. As nature intended, animal skin is very adaptable: not only does leather improve

ABOVE I can almost smell texture. Perhaps it is because the image of a texture in the mind brings the object closer, makes it more real, positions you so closely that you sense its scent. When wood is cerused, its grain becomes whiter and there is greater contrast with its darkness. Even light oaks become more grainy when cerused, and the texture seems deeper. This rather diminutive but pretty bowl arrangement, with its curiously out-of-proportion flowers, exaggerates the earthiness of the wood.

BELOW More flowers, this time stylized in the form of a table by Paris-based designer Hubert Le Gall. Not only is the curve of the flower motif highlighted by the geometry of the cut-pile rug behind, by Christine Van Der Hurd, but the two very different textures are also dramatized very effectively by their juxtaposition: the coarseness of the metal and the depth of the rug's pile.

with age, it also suits different climates and rarely looks unkempt. When leather is used for seating, or on floor or walls, it is durable and a good base texture. It is also of boundless value as an accent, sitting well with both rough-hewn and smooth walls, metal furniture, lacquerwork, raffia, concrete, and all manner of materials. It can be sueded, polished, stamped, embossed, or perforated, thus giving myriad texture possibilities in itself. Jean-Dominique Bonhotal's Paris duplex (*see* pages 48–49) is an excellent example of variation of texture with leather: the red and black leather chairs and sofa are visually and physically warmed by sheepskin, cashmere, and woolen throws and pale woven-wood wall panels.

Texture can sometimes be the starting point for an entire building, as in the decision to build in wood, concrete, or

RIGHT A good texture combination can make the difference between a good home and a great home. Imagine the gulf between an Abstract Expressionist painting and a color-photocopy pastiche of the same painting. There is no comparison between the two. Some people live without sight, others without hearing, but no one should have to live without touch.

FAR RIGHT Compound texturing can be delicious. The contrast of the metal against the oak has been further developed here by using woven metal, which adds to the overall texture. It is often said that the creation of a room is not about painting a picture but creating a collage. A room has so many vertical, horizontal, and other flat surfaces—a wealth of opportunity for surface texture. Most of us find comfort and satisfaction in the cool touch of metal, which comes from underground, and the warmth of wood that grows above it.

brick. Of course, like most of the elements in a classic interior, it cannot be treated as an unrelated topic, but must be considered as part of the whole. In particular, in interior design as in the natural world, texture cannot be viewed separately from color, since it is possible to achieve a variety of different surface effects in a single colorway, which will appear to be rather different hues and cannot by any means be taken as "matching." When planning a scheme of texture and color, do not be swept away by emotion alone: consider the colors and non-colors in terms of textiles, paint, stains, leathers, woods, marble, metals, wall treatments such as stucco, and furniture finishes such as craquelure.

In designing lighting, the skilled use of texture can be an invaluable problem-solver: backgrounds finished in a darker color will gain emphasis if they are given some texture, whereas objects in a pale, highly reflective color will be enhanced if they are smooth and shiny. Shiny surfaces increase light reflectance (*see page 82*) while matte or toothy textures soak up light and decrease reflectance. By maximizing these differences in the amount of reflected light the designer can maximize (or minimize) brightness contrast and the visual impact of a room.

It is often nature that gives the greatest insight into texture. Interior designer Jonathan Reed (*see pages 20–21*) spent his childhood in Yorkshire in the north of England, where he found inspiration for both his color and his texture palettes: "the slate, dry-stone walls, the look of the rain beating the stone" are etched on his mind, he says. He also believes texture to be more important than color in his interiors—"the worked stone with the unworked stone, the shiny and the matt, the velvet with the silk." The texture "palette" is particularly

important to Jonathan Reed since he works within a very muted and neutral color palette. The early-twentieth-century American architect Louis Sullivan suggested we should design buildings the same way: "We must turn again to Nature, and hearkening to her melodious voice, learn as children learn the accent of its rhythmic cadences."

We all have our favorite textures, as we have preferred colors. My own are vellum (not only for its feel, but also for its translucency and elegant ivory-like color) and slate (for its visual texture and color, as well as touch); having seen slate in the context of Brittany in northwestern France, where the land is flat and the sea nearby, I find the combination of elements there thought-provoking, and tend to use slate on floors with sea-green hues nearby. I also love many kinds of wood, including hardwoods such as teak, and softwoods to accessorize—for instance, the very gentle pear wood, often used as framework in seventeenth- and eighteenth-century French furniture, but nowadays more prohibitive costwise and found in details such as the door handles produced by craftsman Paul Belvoir. Cerused woods, for example, oaks, are always delicious, and well deserved their favor with French furniture designers of the 1940s. *Stucco de Venezia* is a wall effect I find utterly elegant (the pigment is mixed with stone dust, marble dust or similar textured material, but the total effect is smooth to touch, and lightly but definitely speckled), as I do *tadelak*, the Moroccan equivalent, in which subtle shiny swirls are only detectable in certain lights. Any metal has potential for beauty, depending upon how it has been worked and the form it takes (the furniture of Diego Giacometti comes to mind)—its patina, too. But my absolute desire is for black lacquer. As the Japanese say, it has

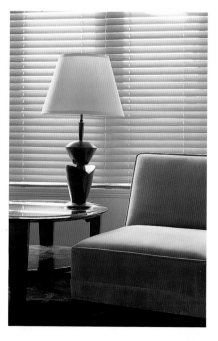

LEFT, TOP Cashmere in a bedroom can be chic, luxurious, and warm. The combination of the pillow and bed cover, the black-painted metal bar of the bed frame (and its skinniness), and the woven wooden wall is quite dramatic yet enticing. In summer the fabric can be changed to linen, silk, or cotton, giving equal depth to the texture relationship.

LEFT Ceramics, a paper-fold-finish table, and a wool pile carpet against a concrete floor: a mix of temperatures, texture, and form. Smooth, glazed ceramics would not be as successful in this grouping, nor would a textured metal table. The harmony between the satin-finished table and the ridges of the vases makes this arrangement work.

LEFT, BOTTOM Not all texture combinations have to be breathtakingly bold: subtle ones may be successful, too. Velvet and cut-pile fabrics have always been deemed high-quality and regal, even though some are not. Velvets can be cotton, silk or, my clear favorite, mohair (perhaps because I find myself living in a cool climate these days). Whichever you choose, make sure the quality is more than adequate for the job to be done. A bedroom chair will not receive as much use as a dining or living-room chair, and cotton velvet is quite acceptable and comfortable in any climate. Corduroy is not only robust, but can be quite charming, too.

RIGHT Designers working within a neutral color palette often prefer to maximize textural content. I have always disagreed with the notion of choosing only three main colors when selecting a scheme for a home or an outfit: there are no hard-and-fast rules about how many of anything can be used. Creating a beautiful interior is massively more complicated than any step-by-step accounting system, in the same way as a hothouse bears no relation to a rainforest in its capacity for texture. In this Collett-Zarzycki room, a pair of chairs and their pillows already offer five textures.

many depths. A black-lacquered wall with achromatic art in kaolin on creased canvas by Piero Manzoni is, to my mind, the ultimate in textural contrast and the epitome of elegance.

Some of the most distinguished and sensitive architecture of the twentieth century—and some of the most texture-conscious—can be found at London's Regent's Park Zoo. Berthold Lubetkin (1901–90), the pioneer of the Modern movement in Britain and a believer in building design as an instrument of social progress, was a master of texture or textural differences within one context— and some of the inhabitants to benefit from his magnificent structures and schemes were not even human. His zoological pavilions, commissioned by Tecton in the 1930s, were incredibly significant historically, as their appearance gave the British public its first "hands-on," and unavoidable, experience of Modern architecture and the materials it favored, such as concrete. For Lubetkin, beyond the mixed benefits of its social impact, the zoo work also provided an ideal vehicle through which to explore a neglected aspect of Modernism: the question of man's place in nature.

According to one naturalist, the result "exploded with an impact which changed the zoo from a dull menagerie to an exciting and interesting world where animals really lived." It was part of the power of Lubetkin's architectural genius that his use of contrasting textures drew the inhabitants of his buildings into different environments within the spaces.

The textures incorporated into the pavilions exhibit fascinating contrasts. In the Gorilla House, a metal drum cage with a revolving wall and roof encases a concrete floor, which becomes a warmer hardwood block floor at the front of the

cages to encourage the gorillas to approach nearer to the public. The Penguin Pool, an aquatic sculpture and engineering capriccio, is a delightful ramp affair, and a triumph of carpentry as much as of concrete. The first experiment with reinforced concrete in Britain, it has proven to be one of the most attractive ever.

The adaptability of material combinations in Lubetkin's work translated beautifully through to his work for humans, too, on both practical and aesthetic levels. The interior that he built for himself, in Highpoint Two in north London, is now home to furniture designer Ou Baholyodin. Beneath a graceful parabolic vault painted light blue are gathered a rich variety of materials, textures, shapes, objects, and images, in keeping with Lubetkin's own original approach. A Modernist with a fantasist's mind, Lubetkin chose chunky Norwegian fir wood for the walls to represent a forest, blue to represent sky, and brown stone floors to represent earth.

Every architect has had their enthusiasm dampened by prophetic visions of incongruous furniture filling rooms that are architecturally beautiful. Most people prefer to select their own furniture and personal objects, so that the interior of their house bears the imprint of their personality. But we should not overdo it: each piece should be appropriate, in itself and as part of the whole. Architect Carlos Aparicio knows not to add insignificant bibelots—all elements in his home are welcome attractions.

ELEMENTS

Each element of an interior has its own form: it must be successful both aesthetically and functionally. Designers are answerable to the demands of culture and technology, but in the expression of form they are also free to communicate their own personalities and concepts; their foremost responsibility is to create form that is meaningful.

SHELL

Creation of an interior must inevitably begin with the shell. The walls, ceiling, floor, and doors that contain a space are fundamental: it is just not possible to produce a successful interior by inserting a "look" into an inappropriate shell, and if that desired look is a classic, a sense of suitable context is all the more essential. The architecture of the structure does, of course, set the underlying tone, but in viewing the shell of an interior on an elemental level, it is vital to look beyond the architecture and consider how different wall, ceiling, and floor treatments may affect impressions of the architecture, and our feelings and behavior inside it.

This may take many forms. For example, ceilings, or our impression of them, can be "heightened" by devices such as creating narrower windows, thus making walls seem taller, or "lowered" through the use of suspended lighting to create a platform above head level, or by widening windows. In shaping the shell of a space, the architect or designer can also direct movement. In the nave of a Gothic cathedral, for instance, the high walls confining us closely on both sides urge us to advance along the nave toward the altar and to gaze up into the vaulting overhead, and we feel a sense of exultation and physical release. A vaulted ceiling or double-height room in a contemporary scheme can offer the same sense of exultation, thus the lofty room is often a symbol suggesting achievement and success. Renaissance use of space was entirely different, architects attempting to balance the suggested

movement by drawing people toward a focal point at which they could sense an equilibrium of movement in all directions. With this device we feel physically at rest —in contrast to the experience in the cathedral. This concept has translated through history, as has the Gothic concept, and even the Modernists, who are rarely considered to have been inspired by the Renaissance, showed a preference for low ceilings and a sense of balanced wellbeing.

Different floor finishes in an interior, depending upon their relative proportions, can direct potential movement around a space and can serve to suggest discrete definitions within it. As an example, Terry Hunziker in Seattle (*see* pages 46–47) achieves the sense of a hallway, a suggestion of a elegant passageway through his otherwise open-plan home, by recessing an elongated panel of steel into the floor. One feels bound to tread its path. His windows were also narrowed to increase the perceived height of the room, so in a sense the whole experience is more Gothic than Renaissance. Although it is a thoroughly modern home, it does not follow many of the principles of the Modernists at all and, for its differences alone, possesses in my opinion one of the most enduring styles of our time.

The principles of designing a classic interior apply as much to the shell as to every other element; as always, the most successful designs are those that form a cohesive whole appropriate to the personal taste of the occupant, the architecture, and the other aspects of the design itself.

The old floor of this 1854 New York house has been replaced by an elegant combination of bleached and wire-brushed oak and brown slate, and the entire stairwell has been resculpted into a sweep of scale and grandeur. The Veneziano-stuccoed walls are right for this Italianate house, but are probably a lighter color than they would have been in the nineteenth century.

RIGHT A sliding partition between casual family rooms and an informal dining room becomes a photographic gallery, with a collection of commissioned photographs by Ed Dimsdale hanging one above another and side by side, recessed into panels within the sliding doors. More are recessed into the panels of closet doors. The effect is reminiscent of a traditional print room, a relatively informal room where prints were applied directly to walls. The wooden hood stretching across the ceiling serves to contain the "gallery" and gives it greater visual fluidity.

WALLS AND CEILINGS

The most classic and chic walls are often the simplest, painted or treated in some subtly textured form. The key, of course, is to choose the right combinations of color, light, and texture, and to take into account the complex effects of these variables (*see* pages 60–67 and 74–91).

The simplest wall treatment visually for a classic home, and perhaps the most durable (in both senses: lasting impression and sustainable material) is plaster, troweled or stucco. Stucco swirls are not easily achieved by the non-professional, but the effect is a dream on expanses of wall and a perfect backdrop to sophisticated texture and color.

However, walls are very personal things, and a surprising range of options can work well. A suggestion for, say, flock wallpaper might send some reeling, but in the right hands it can be elegant. Similarly, highly decorative wall treatments—specialized paint effects, beautifully painted friezes, elaborate frescoes—can be the most exquisite icing on a tasty cake, if executed in masterly fashion. One wrong move and the cake becomes a mud pie.

Stripes are a case in point. On dresses, broad bands around even a svelte figure make it seem shorter and fatter; a narrow vertical stripe is elongating. Vertical stripes of varying widths and colors are good for harmonizing proportions. The same applies to the home.

In Jean-Dominique Bonhotal's dining room (*see* page 69), the curvature created on one wall is counterbalanced by the opposing wall, where the center is painted in dramatic vertical stripes a few inches wide, in two complementary colors. In addition to helping balance the room, the stripes add a formal accent to its informal tone. They also conceal the fact that it once held a fireplace; the curved wall on one side and stripes on the other shift the focus toward the window wall in between.

The French have always been fond of a stripe or two, and when I lived in Paris, I liked to mark the

BELOW Jean-Dominique Bonhotal's bedroom is all about texture and simplicity. Containing little but a bed and two chairs, it suggests a hint of the Orient. The room derives its flavor and character from the large panels of woven wood that serve as walls; if the walls were painted, the effect would be entirely different and quite plain. The furniture is incidental but correct.

RIGHT A small room in an apartment where the two principal rooms are vast has been turned into a library (with the books on each side of the entrance). Seen from the hall, the enticing paneling is stylish and controlled, suggesting repose and study. The framing of the architectural drawing is very modern, but it is hung by an old English method—it is wholly European to hang pictures on chains, ropes, or visible wires.

OPPOSITE This dining room's fireplace chimney has been covered over and obscured by a wall painted with stripes in tones of mahogany and red. Three apartments have become one: none of the rooms serves its original purpose and not all elements need remain. Closing off the fireplace has allowed the terrace and park views to dominate (a dining room generally needs only a table as a focal point, but these gardens are very fine). The sculpture is a nineteenth-century reproduction of the Venus de Milo.

arrival of summer by wandering through the Palais Royal at that divine moment when the taupe-and-white striped awnings are let down. It is said that men like bold stripes, women narrow; those at the Palais Royal are sexless and perfect in their proportions. The popularity of stripes in the English Regency and French Directoire and Empire periods may have been due in part to weaving methods and regulations, which meant that stripes were less expensive than complicated damasks and brocades (prints were banned to combat the threat of imported Indian calico).

Stripes remain chic, unfussy, and useful. As American designer Michael Greer put it, they are

"putty in your designer's hand." Paris-based interior designer Frédéric Méchiche has made the stripe his signature. In a recent scheme, broad stripes of different widths in related pastel hues were painted from floor to ceiling, across the ceiling and down the opposite wall, giving the effect of a spacious, arched cocoon. The room is both cozy and lofty.

Even striped floors can look good if stripes are used at right angles to the axis to make a narrow room seem wider. The same is true of ceilings; in fact, stripes can improve almost any room. In the form of pilasters, they make a delightful addition to a classical room without space for columns.

Wallpaper—striped or not—has been out of vogue for many decades, but I have not stopped being a fan. Nor has Maureen Paley, who has a passion for historical archive or "document" wallpapers (see page 80). There is no comparison between the upper and lower leagues of wallpaper companies: in this area, cost generally does assure quality.

I also tend to agree with Michael Greer that "A small room... can be made to seem larger and more unified by wallpapering the ceiling with the same paper as the walls.... Muted directional patterns can be satisfactory, but the direction should flow across the ceiling and down the most conspicuous wall."

ABOVE Intermixed surfaces add interest in a room devoid of moldings and other decorative embellishment. These walls are of cement plaster, with steel wainscoting that provides a horizon line around the room. The materials are softened by the fabric of the headboard, and further textures are introduced by the woods.

Fabric-covered walls (*see* page 92) can be extremely chic. The fabric may be stretched onto frames before being applied to walls in panels, the French way, or pasted on directly. Jonathan Reed's interiors are often blessed with this detail, his use of materials quite original: he favors burlap and linen—or any fabric with good texture or slub. Fabric walls are often a way to "warm up" a room and add a new dimension to furniture, since they have a relationship with upholstery.

Wood paneling can be warming and give the effect of enclosure if dark woods are used; with lighter woods, such as light oak, bleached teak, elm, or maple, it tends to be

refreshing. Paneling is generally symmetrical and adds to the order of a room. With imagination, it may become the main feature, as in the bedroom of Jean-Dominique Bonhotal (*see* page 95), with its woven-wood wall panels. It may also change character seasonally, as in the Belgian maritime penthouse designed by Andrée Putman (*see* pages 38–39), where teak paneling is echoed in waxed teak floors.

As for moldings, architraves, and other embellishments, these must be guided by architecture and personal preference. Maureen Paley deliberately embellished her cottage in London's East End with gilded moldings and architraves that would not have been

considered right when it was built, since it was meant to be, well, basic. The East End is now somewhat more salubrious than in the nineteenth century, and her personalized additions work very well. However, there is no hard-and-fast rule. An unadorned dress can be just as attractive as an adorned one; the decision depends upon spirit and occasion. No one could imagine a molding in Philip Johnson's Glass House in New Canaan, Connecticut. Nor could we conceive of the Russian baroque Catherine Palace in St. Petersburg, where lintel panels are richly carved and gilded, and crimson pilasters are set behind glass, without such ornamentation.

LEFT Specialized paint effects can be laborious, but are well worth the effort. Expert Richard Clark works with Collett-Zarzycki to find the right pigment to suit a room's color scheme. This large drawing room has walls in what is termed "linen finish", created by pigmenting, then scratching back the plaster. In this case, it was just left there. Sometimes the experts go further, glazing then applying polish to create a shinier effect.

BELOW Glazing walls, instead of just painting, is no vainglorious extravagance: they last a great deal longer. Glazed and matte walls react differently to light, and shiny ones are more noticeable than matte of the same color. Stucco and the Moroccan version, *tadelak*, are very warming if polished. Some designers like high-gloss automotive-spray paint because of its ease of application (true lacquering takes an age). The prosaic should not be sniffed at.

DOORS

Early doors, with pivots at one side fitting into sockets in sill and head, came into being in ancient Egypt; in the twelfth century, pivoting was replaced by hinges. These offered opportunity for decoration, with wrought-iron hinge plates hammered into scrolls. The late Renaissance saw the advent of the framed and paneled door.

The grandest doors are made of finely figured hardwood—mahogany and rosewood—but heavy, solid doors now tend to be avoided in favor of those with a softwood core or a structure covered by sheets of veneer. Metal doors are now viable, too, since they can be lightweight. There is also scope for finishes, even with simple lines: doors can be painted or lacquered, covered with felt or fabric, leather, or mirror.

Hinged doors, hung well, can make for a dramatic room entrance; a doorway offers anticipation of delights within. The door must be weighty enough for substance, light enough to work without effort. Sliding doors are wonderful, since they escape into walls rather than encumbering a room that might otherwise need more girth.

Door heights are like chairs: the taller suggest grandeur, the shorter discretion (Beverly Hills boasts some of the tallest front doors imaginable!). My preference is for sliding interior doors with a mechanism at the top only, so the floor is uninterrupted.

BELOW Doors are one of the few features of interiors that should be either conspicuous or inconspicuous, but not left somewhere in between. These sanded glass doors disappear entirely when not required and allow light through when closed. There is no runner along the floor, but the mechanism is well balanced and the doors glide easily.

BOTTOM Some doors melt into walls as barely discernible panels. Handles are not always necessary: a door can be pressed and spring open. These majestic mirrored closet doors are too heavy for such mechanisms and look as if they ache to be pulled. The handles help the mirror blend with the room's neutral tones and natural textures.

LEFT We imagine that a door to a closet or bathroom should be less conspicuous. This is not always so, especially with lateral living, where it is essential to keep up the standard of stylishness since most areas of the home may be visible on entry. In Sally Sirkin Lewis's single-story home, black "lacquer" doors mark all doorways, including this one to a washroom.

BELOW It has become fashionable to lose all decorative moldings unless of great historical significance, but while the picture moulding is a happy loss, in some classical houses ceiling moldings and baseboards may be attractive or architecturally essential. In a neoclassical home, decorative architraves around doors can give an added dimension to otherwise flat surfaces.

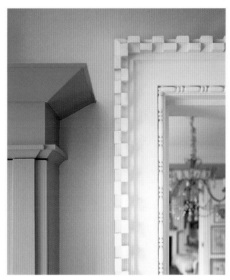

BELOW Folding copper-mesh-fronted doors concealing a small room disappear further when folded, by sliding into the walls. The floor is uninterrupted, with no tracks for the doors. Accordion and folding screen doors are not new: in 1954, Gio Ponti incorporated his "Modernfold" doors into his own home to section off his mother's and daughter's rooms, and to hide closets.

LEFT Sliding doors benefit from not having a handle. Door furniture can be recessed or, simpler still, holes can be made in doors to pull them apart, and no floor space needs to be left in front of them. Be sure you want sliding doors before installing them: it may seem attractive to have two rooms that can be one, but few people make full use of the flexibility. They are useful, however, between living and dining rooms that are often combined for entertaining.

RIGHT The latticework on this wall is a trick to make the eye believe the wall is just a wall: the three columns are in fact closet doors, which pop open when pressed on one side. Fortunately, these doors conceal treasured flatware and porcelain that is not in everyday use. For a storage area in continual use, it would be wiser to have better protection from fingerprints, such as easy-to-polish metal surfaces.

LEFT An unusual bleached and wire-brushed brown slate and oak floor. Slate is generally a fairly soft stone (depending upon region), very stable, and easy to work and shape. It varies in color from dark blue to heather colors and gray-green. Formed in layers, it can be machined very flat and is easily split, making it suitable for floors and roofing. It is beautiful and easy to care for (use linseed and turpentine mix), but expensive.

RIGHT Textures, more than anything else, foster a style: massive wooden staircases and beamed ceilings would only be at home in the country, but slate and stone floors (here, gray slate), with whitewash and natural woods, can be used anywhere, including in the chicest of townhouses. Like other nonporous floors—ceramic and quarry tile—slate is impervious to most household liquids. Nonporous floors are usually the most durable and hard-wearing.

FAR RIGHT Traditional parquet floors are made up of short strips of hardwood laid in a herringbone, basket, or brick pattern, either individually or glued in panels premounted on plywood. Parquet floors are mightily attractive on their own. The hardwood is, of course, hardy, and the floors improve with age. As an alternative, you may find existing wooden boards in your home—usually of softwood: fir, spruce, or pine. Boards can be sanded and sealed. Colored with pigmented translucent wood sealer or with a water-based stain, they make a good base for islands of rugs.

FLOORS

The "terra firma" beneath our feet, physically and psychologically, floors can make or break a scene. Their construction can be problematic, too. Concrete floors will support any flooring, but you cannot lay, for example, quarry tiles on domestic wood suspended floors without advice on floor load.

The most classic-looking floors are *parquet de Versailles* and black-and-white squares (tile or marble). Both give scope for islands of rugs: traditional Aubusson or Savonnerie, or cotton-bordered sisal, jute, or coir. Marble, the classicists' choice, is now rather costly; terrazzo—marble chippings set in cement—is a hardwearing alternative. Very hard floors can be tiring to stand on, however, and ceramic tiles and stone can be noisy underfoot.

Some of the loveliest residences have basic wooden floors which, if re-laid, sanded, sealed, and finished, may become the veritable silk purse from the sow's ear. Otherwise, they are best covered.

Carpeting is not always a good look, but it can be if it is of good quality and its color enhances the scene (*see* pages 14–15), or if its pattern dictates a scheme, as in the geometric carpets of the late David Hicks. Wall-to-wall floor covering gives a room foundation.

Concrete, while prosaic, can have an elegant, confident, and unifying effect (*see* pages 36–37). Slate is even-temperatured and durable, its depth of color forming a versatile backdrop. Above all, flooring must unify a space. It is the map that plots a home's journey.

RIGHT The black-and-white checkerboard laid on a diagonal is always rated highly as a classic floor, especially if marble. Although invented much earlier, it was held in great esteem by even the Victorians, whose taste was often dubious! Marble is extremely hard-wearing and can come in many colors. It has unparalleled beauty, to my mind, and is easy to care for (but can be slippery when wet). It must be laid in a cement bed on a concrete subfloor.

FAR RIGHT Concrete screed (sand and cement screed over a concrete floor) has become the mantra for the new industrial loft home, and has some great advantages. It is perfect for underfloor heating, which I hope will become more and more common in temperate climates, since it is less obtrusive and more attractive than heating grilles and radiators. Concrete screed expands and contracts, so lines must be scored in it so that it cracks "naturally" along them and not at random. Smaller slabs crack less.

LEFT A see-through fireplace, where back-to-back fireplaces have been cleverly converted into one, warms both sides of a reapportioned room. It has become popular to knock through two rooms, retaining the chimney frame and fireplace. In this apartment, however, the fireplace has been created completely anew using adzed Portland stone and slate. The perforated metal lamp is by John and Silvia Reid, the chair a modern classic by Charles Eames that, despite its modishness in re-edition, is a sound acquisition (especially if it is an original) and very practical.

RIGHT, ABOVE A basic but attractive fireplace in Portland stone and slate—materials that are signatures of Jonathan Reed's work—dresses down a London apartment whose embellishments already include ceiling moldings. Too much frou-frou cannot be good for you. Many designers today spend time designing the "logs" in gas-fire grates for maximum realism.

RIGHT Some fireplaces should be left as you find them. Any city of character abounds in such elements, and many older houses have delightful fireplaces. Carlos Aparicio found lovely surprises in this Manhattan apartment. Fireplaces original to period rooms are usually of the right scale (if sometimes overdecorated). The mantel is quite high by today's standards, making the small French furniture, such as the exquisitely pretty chair by Emile Ruhlmann in the foreground, seem even more demure.

FIREPLACES

Traditionally, the fireplace was the focal point of a room (even, in a sense, a kind of household altar). From the late 1950s the television took over this role, but today fireplaces are returning to prominence, as televisions and movie screens merit their own room. Some rooms require a fireplace as a focal point; others do not. I often think of fireplaces as handbags: practical or brazen, they are not always necessary, but can act as a comfort or distraction.

There is nothing lovelier than a period fireplace – perhaps Adam or Louis XV – in many situations. Prestigious mantelpieces are carved from white or intricately veined marble, or from porphyry. Others are created in limestone, slate, granite, sandstone, and one of my favorites, scagliola. Quality mantels are equally attractive with new decorative schemes and in classical interiors. The low-slung fireplace, a recess in the wall with no embellishment, is ironically less easy to work with aesthetically: it rarely blends with period furniture and can look unfinished – yet may be extremely effective in a seamless pared-down space.

If a room has a fireplace and stunning views, the ideal is to make the fireplace the focal point in winter and evenings, while the windows take over in summer. In the seafront apartment designed by Andrée Putman (see pages 38–39), attention is redirected by closing off the fireplace with glass doors.

Air circulation affects fire quality, as does room size, and fires tend not to work well if rooms are knocked together, unless adapted. Expert advice may be needed.

Choice of fireplace has much to do with where you live. Real-looking natural-gas fires have come a long way, and both contemporary and traditional rooms can benefit from the ease, warmth, and beauty of the flames.

LEFT A newly created and installed fireplace is accurately drawn from a fireplace design by Thomas Hope (1769–1831), whose talents inspired Sir John Soane, a man of impeccable taste. The limestone fireplace has stars and a geometric design in blue infill: although many people think stars were born in the 1980s, or at least alongside Post-Modernism, these stars are original to the eighteenth-century design and happen to be an old motif. Perhaps the new art makes us see the fireplace's beginnings differently.

ABOVE If your house is old and you are going to furnish a room in a fairly formal manner, a fireplace can provide the fulcrum about which the room is balanced. Since it is better to keep consistency in the main architectural features of a room, if you replace an old fireplace with a new one, make sure you look at paneled doors and sash windows at the same time: one or both may need replacing, too. It is rare that an older-style fireplace works well in a new house, unless particularly impressive (and I don't mean grand) in its design. Architectural salvage companies can advise.

LEFT If you have an opportunity to make a statement, why not go all out? Not many homes could take such gigantic proportions, but this floor-to-ceiling fireplace, in steel sheeting over a frame box, appears as a section of wall, a welcome accent in the enormity of white space. The fireplace itself is not vast, but supplements the room's underfloor heating.

FURNITURE

ABOVE A northern European neoclassical chair and a table by the Baguès brothers in bronze and red lacquer, dating from around the 1930s. The writer Laurie Lee once said that a poet should not read his own work: it needs another's interpretation. When assembling furniture for a room, we have the advantage of time over those who created pieces for a particular era, and the luxury of being able to select from many different periods. A classic room need not contain only furniture based on classical lines—although this can be the finest. Whatever you select, try to understand the intentions of the pieces' creators, then reinterpret them for modern living.

OPPOSITE The "Tonneau Table," which I think looks like a mushroom, is part of a collection by Christian Liaigre. It has a wooden base and limestone top: the combination of materials—warm base with cooler stone—and the form of the piece are highly unusual. We have come a long way since architects felt a piece of furniture needed to be designed as part of the whole scheme, and the curator who collates and displays art and furniture may sometimes achieve better results than the artist who creates it.

Architects tend to see themselves as responsible for molding the lives of the people who live in their buildings, and there is something utopian in their thinking when they design furniture to fit their interiors. William Morris, Antoni Gaudí, Frank Lloyd Wright, and Le Corbusier, to name but a few, all considered it their right to design every aspect of a building, inside and out, and in doing so they felt they were making the world a better place. Our instincts may rebel, but in the words of Oscar Wilde, "A map of the world that does not include Utopia is not worth glancing at, for it leaves out the one country at which Humanity is always landing."

Although we have been blessed with the work of these architects, they are an adventurous minority, and we do not have to follow suit. They have changed our way of looking at a chair, for example, as Picasso changed our way of looking at painting, but few of us live with collections of Picasso's paintings, or would wish to.

There is no single type of good-quality furniture. In addition to looking instinctively good, it must be well made, durable, have the right "pitch," and work well. Design and our requirements of it have become increasingly complex, but tubular steel, even gently bent plywood, can hardly replace the time-worn patina of handcrafted furniture, lovingly made by generations of cabinetmakers. And we should not expect it to. Modern times have modern manners. Some twenty-first-century designers do remain faithful to the carpentry standards of the past: David Linley produces furniture exclusively

in England, and keeps many craftspeople in employment creating desks, tables, and all sorts of home accessories in luxury woods such as macassar ebony and rippled sycamore. But Linley's vision is rare, although his marquetry will undoubtedly become the collectors' pieces of the future.

Today we have the advantage of living in a time when fine Georgian furniture can still be found; travel is no longer exclusive to the rich (so we can source odd objects the world over); and we have an understanding of the ideals both of past architects and of modern furniture designers, and can take our pick. Most importantly, we have a plethora of stores and galleries educating us and attuning our eyes to "good" design, so home design can become a matter of taste. We have, for the most part, well-seasoned critics, too.

Even in the past ten years, as I have been following architecture, art, and design through journalistic work, things have changed. There are more knowledgeable people in the field willing to share their thoughts; design schools are offering more specialized and diverse courses; and imaginative homes are photographed and exposed more often. Advances in technology have meant that design is forever changing as new techniques become commonplace. The standards may not be the same as those of the past, but they are standards nonetheless. The quality of machine-made furniture is improving, and the options are enormous, but we do at least have a choice, and we have to learn to trust in our education and instincts.

SEATING

A chair should be elegant in form without displaying grandeur: whether designed by William Kent, Robert Adam, Frank Lloyd Wright, or Le Corbusier, the best are demure, "seen and not heard." It must also have the right level of ergonomic comfort or pitch.

As an architect, R. M. Schindler (*see* page 70) understood the importance of a chair's scale, its placement and, above all, its comfort and functionality. As he put it, "Only lately have we again discovered the real height and breadth of a human being. Ceilings shelter us instead of crowning our position. Doors are to walk through rather than to form an impressive frame for one who carefully pauses on the threshold. The chair supports the back rather than producing an aura for our head."

A chair that won great acclaim in the late 1990s was the limited-edition "HK 97," commissioned from London-based Ou Baholyodhin for the ceremony to mark Hong Kong's return to China. Made of steel, it followed the low lines typical of the Ming dynasty (1368–1644), and in its simplicity looked both ancient and modern, a true classic.

Sofas and upholstered chairs are the royal family of the living room, and should embody the comfort and deep-seated ease of our century. Too often, upholstered sofas are bought with the emphasis on appearance—fabric, color, line and design—when workmanship and hidden materials are the key to quality and comfort. The durability of the frame depends upon the way

ABOVE Zebra skin has become a classic for rugs, but is not often found as upholstery. This new chair follows Chippendale lines: early Georgian upholstered chairs usually had plain, overstuffed seats and backs, and part-padded arms. Chippendale's *Director* catalog includes examples of French-inspired armchairs with light, graceful legs. The combination of zebra and "Georgian" chair is highly effective in a modern home.

BELOW A set of unusual stools with zoomorphic feet. The zoomorphic or animal leg and foot is my absolute favorite, especially if it has a knee or hoof. These stools have both. Animal feet are ancient: Tutankhamen's carved wooden chair (fourteenth century B.C., from Thebes) had animal feet; the Romans favored claws.

OPPOSITE

TOP LEFT David Roland's 1964 award-winning compact stacking chair in chromed steel, with back and seat in black enameled sheet steel, also slots together laterally. Forty can be stacked to a height of only 4 feet (1.2 meters), hence its name, GF 40/4.

TOP CENTER These stools can be used for sitting, as footstools, or as incidental tables. Based on stools found in Tutankhamen's tomb, copies of these designs are still found in modern-day Cairo. The opening of the tombs in the 1920s caused quite an impact worldwide: many "1920s-looking" pieces had their inception in ancient Egypt.

TOP RIGHT A sleek design by Holly Hunt draws on a chair from circa 1800 by Sheraton, who specialized in straight backs. This chair shows a mix of influences, with arms joined to the seat in Chippendale manner, rather than to the front legs.

LEFT The Greek *klismos* chair, armless with a slightly curved back and plain, inwardly curved legs, evolved into the Roman *cathedra* and then became a blueprint for some Georgian chairs, as here; the neoclassical revival in the 1940s revived its popularity.

CENTER Based on origami, the abstract "Chair" (1991) is made of welded and folded "hematite"-patinated sheet steel. Designer Michael Wolfson wanted to defy the definition of "chair" as "a seat for one person usually with four legs, a back and sometimes arms."

RIGHT These Russian birchwood chairs from circa 1815 have a sobriety and elegance often found in fine Russian furniture of the nineteenth century. With its craftsmanship and intriguing styles, Russian furniture blends well with modern.

BOTTOM LEFT French Louis XV style has become almost standard worldwide in chic homes. Louis XV, with its shell and scroll motif, is distinguished from the later Louis XVI style by cabriole legs and a more rounded form. A contemporary fabric tends to throw the chair into a less formal mood.

BOTTOM CENTER Philippe Starck's three-legged "Dr. Sonderbar" (1983) is particularly refined in its spindliness and low back. With no formal design training, Starck has produced highly original and sculptural chairs that happily stand alone.

BOTTOM RIGHT French furniture owes its quality to a demand for perfection from an informed clientele and skilled craftsmen protected by guilds. In nineteenth-century France, many influences came together and could be selected at will.

the wood has been dried and fitted together, as well as on the webbing or other foundation.

Upholstered furniture developed in Europe during the seventeenth century; at first, pieces were heavy and awkward. (The word "sofa" derives from the Arabic *suffah*, meaning a cushion on a camel's saddle.) By the mid-eighteenth century, the French and English had refined sofas and chairs into light, graceful creations, whose style has stood the test of time.

The sofa is the most-used piece of furniture, the center of conversational groups, and needs two or three upholstered satellite chairs if the room is to be truly comfortable. These elements do not have to match in color or form, although an underlying theme often works best. A brightly colored baroque chaise longue can harmonize with square-cushioned seating if, perhaps, the colors are related, or if there is another baroque element in the room. Upholstered furniture not only comforts, but feels solid—colored or black sofas can anchor a room. Sofas and easy chairs need not be plump, but subtle curves do soften harsh lines elsewhere. Because of their size and key role, and the importance of circulation, sofas should always be included in any template of a room plan.

OPPOSITE

TOP LEFT A very handsome pair of chairs following a 1940s line, their backs and arms one continuous height. If arms are too high, there is no point in having them, since they box the sitter in. While comfortable, these chairs are not for lounging in, since the backs reach only to waist height. As occasional chairs, they work extremely well, partly because their height does not disrupt the balance of the room.

TOP RIGHT A four-seater sofa is more useful than a three-seater, since three-seaters only ever accommodate two: a third person feels like piggy-in-the-middle. The other advantage is that two people can sit at each end with their legs to the center.

LEFT A red leather-upholstered armchair, "Vivette" by Luca Meda for Molteni, is a new "off-the-shelf" variety. Sofas and armchairs, unlike other furniture in a new classic home, are not likely to be custom-designed since there are many good, suitably proportioned pieces on the market.

CENTER "Sofa" today refers to any plump, upholstered, elongated chair; "settee" denotes a more spindly, less upholstered affair. Settee was the original word, however, for an extended chair used for sitting rather than reclining. The European variety dates from the mid-seventeenth century, when it was intended for a single sitter. Early in the eighteenth century, the double or triple form became fashionable.

RIGHT Design classics are becoming as collectable as art, and re-editions by the masters, here by Rietveld, may have to be made to order. Detailed blueprints are adhered to, with no room for additions or alterations to any aspect. Original pieces from the twentieth century are becoming rarer, owing to their recent popularity.

BOTTOM LEFT A black-leather upholstered armchair by current French designer Christian Liaigre could not be more precise in line and form: its pitch is perfect. Although not heavily padded, the chair is comfortable in height and depth, and the head is well supported.

BOTTOM CENTER A rare original masterpiece from the 1940s by Danish designer Fritz Henningsen. The inward and outward curves of the chair's body and the cabriole legs help soften a linear room.

BOTTOM RIGHT A small-scale armchair based on Victorian lounge chairs. From the late nineteenth century, their appearance was lightened by removing the upholstery filling between arms and seat. These chairs are strong and comfortable.

ABOVE A banquette sofa differs from a regular sofa in that it has no arms and is, at least to some extent, built in or attached to the wall (as in many restaurants and diners). The advantage is that it becomes part of the shell of a room, and is not distracting. Banquettes create their own niches just by being there. Needless to say, a banquette must be attractive so it does not end up becoming an apologetic, wallflowerlike seating arrangement.

TABLES

Tables, like chairs, appear throughout the home in many guises. As modern life becomes more complex, we need more surfaces with multiple uses.

Small, rudimentary wooden tables were in use in ancient Egypt; by Roman times they were more common and taller. In the Middle Ages, the forms became rounded.

Today, dining, bedside, and occasional tables are found in most homes; side tables, games tables, and consoles are rarer. The coffeetable, in scale the oldest form, although its use has changed, is particularly useful, acting as a boundary between people in close settings. The choice of table is quite significant, since it takes up space and usually has to be walked around. Like a chair, a table exists as sculpture in miniature.

Height must be the first consideration, particularly for a dining table. How often have table and chairs been acquired separately, only for the owner discover that they do not quite fit together?

Details such as ornamental feet must remain details and not take over the entire look, unless they are making a statement—for example, by adding to a streamlined interior a carved African table or a Brancusi-inspired geometric form. If well incorporated, the latter can lend almost Cubist form to a room.

ABOVE I was fascinated by this graceful glass and metal table, which I assumed, because of its length, came apart in three places. It does not. The delicacy of its line was further enhanced by this discovery. If you look closely, you will see the bar across the bottom that gives the secret away. I also rather like the distortion of the images above, works from a 1996 series, *Portraits* by Harald Dortsmüller, against the precision of the console table.

OPPOSITE

TOP LEFT This vigorous table by Gene Summers has zigzag legs reminiscent of African tribal art. The heavy glass circular top is tinted dark to add to its mystery.

TOP CENTER Although these Chinese-style occasional tables in Cuban mahogany are small, they benefit from having space to breathe. As side tables they are useful; joined in a group of four, they make a stunning coffee table.

TOP RIGHT A circular table is as likely to be found in an entrance hall as a library or living room (ones with drawers are drum tables, meant for storage and writing on in libraries). This late-eighteenth-century English table, with handsome carved feet, is quite at home with good American art.

LEFT A rectangular 1970s table with steel legs, found at a flea market, is home to a "tablescape," a term coined by the late English interior designer David Hicks.

CENTER Remarkable shapes have been inspired by Cubism, particularly by the Romanian sculptor Constantin Brancusi. In the 1920s, Brancusi reached for the essence of things through abstraction: he eliminated detail and concentrated on the character of his model, which might have been a bird.

RIGHT Something between Brancusi-inspired forms and the African-inspired table, this piece's geometric base adds a sculptural element to a corner of a room that is ostensibly for living. It is used more as a gaming table than for dining, but is substantial enough for either.

BOTTOM LEFT A re-edition of an occasional table by Jacques Adnet in oak and bronze hosts a flower vase and Danish bowl with serpent motif. Working in the 1920s–40s, Adnet took a logical, refined approach, applying stark functionalism, yet he believed in subtle ornamentation, and mixed modern design with traditional.

BOTTOM CENTER A wood and metal combination, here oak and forged steel, is attractive in a table. These bedside tables could have looked like wooden boxes with drawers, but the curved metal wall supports (mainly decorative) add sturdiness and echo other metalwork in the home, such as forged-iron curtain poles.

BOTTOM RIGHT No stranger to the complexity of simplicity, Robert Bray designed these heavy steel tables because he liked their industrial tone. Tables are his favorite furniture, and he likes to assess them with other pieces and alone: just by being tables, "they imply their multi-use."

CLOSETS

Closets and armoires tend to be remembered by association rather than appearance. I have childhood memories of the perfumed scent of bathroom closets after my parents had left for a party, and of the desperately enticing odors from the pantry, the pungent smell of orange marmalade and cloves. John Keats obviously had similar recollections in "The Eve of Saint Agnes": "And still she slept an azure-lidded sleep, In blanchèd linen, smooth and lavender'd, While he from the closet brought a heap—Of candied apple, quince, and plum, and gourd." Closets are exciting platforms, proscenium stages, that hold small worlds. In the film *The Great Gatsby*, surely one of the most memorable scenes is when Daisy opens Gatsby's clothes closet to reveal freshly laundered shirts in myriad colors.

Built-in closets sit well in a room only when they are part of the original design, the "total work of art," or when an interior has been completely rethought (*see* page 39). In the home designed by Andrée Putman for Jean-Paul Goude in Paris, closets are even concealed within the bed frame: in a small wenge-wood room, four square pillars appear to support the ceiling at the corners of the bed, but actually provide storage space so the walls are "freed from the banality of closets."

LEFT Palest pink "lacquer" glamorizes a vanity unit containing closets, drawers, and basin. This exceptionally well-groomed bathroom is not huge, but is well organized thanks to this piece of furniture, which appears built-in but is not. The tilting mirror is a desirable addition to any bathroom; here it is part of the unit, saving more space.

OPPOSITE, TOP LEFT The scale and form of this wall-hung cabinet by George Nakashima are intrinsic to the art of the wall. Its vertical slats, horizontal form, and woodenness, coupled with the hanging disks and organic form of the sculpture, attractively balance the whole room. Freeing up floor space adds to the airiness.

OPPOSITE, TOP RIGHT A small cerused-wood cabinet provides convenient storage and a touch of character. Although chunky, its low level keeps it neat, the textured wood echoing the *parquet de Versailles* floor in the dining room of Nye Basham's elegant Paris apartment.

OPPOSITE, RIGHT The unusual "Cubist" cabinet in mahogany veneer, by Michael Wolfson, plays with angles usually confined to art and sculpture. One of a pair, its form takes the traditional edge off a room that includes eighteenth-century Dutch wingback chairs. The cabinet holds a collection of *faux-bois* ceramics from Vallauris.

OPPOSITE, BOTTOM LEFT As its name suggests, the "cupboard" is a descendant of the credence or buffet, a series of open shelves for drinking vessels and tableware. This cabinet in Jenny Armit's Los Angeles home has evolved a long way from those simple boards.

OPPOSITE, BOTTOM CENTER This highly refined custom-made sycamore cabinet takes pride of place in a living room; belying its looks, it accommodates TV, hi-fi, and bar.

OPPOSITE, BOTTOM RIGHT Many cupboards are today used very differently from their original purpose (such as metal military closets now used for clothing). In its former life in the early twentieth century, this clothing cabinet was an industrial safe, from Blackman-Cruz.

BEDS

Whoever heard of a "design classic" bed from the twentieth century? There were some ultra "designed" beds in the 1960s and '70s, but I am not sure that they would be accepted now. In the late 1950s, Italian furniture designer Joe Colombo designed a couple of extraordinary bed-living modular pieces in an attempt to create an "integral habitat": the "Rotoliving" and "Cabriolet-Bed" were remarkable experiments in form and injection-molded plastic, telling a tale of their time, but they could in no way be considered classics of today.

Some designers produce interesting beds on traditional lines, including four-posters, which can be very attractive. Otherwise, beds are best custom-designed to meet occupants' requirements, and should not be too fashionable, nor too fussy. A four-poster bed can be handsome if it is kept to Ming-like lines (see right), but not if draped in swathes of dusty fabric. Except for futon-inspired designs, I feel beds should not be too low: beds that cannot be jumped down from are often somehow depressing.

Bed linen can make all the difference to comfort. Egyptian cotton or linen sheets, generous pillows and bolsters, and cashmere or raw-silk throws make chic additions to any bed. Other bedroom paraphernalia should be kept to a minimum, concealed in drawers or bedside cabinets.

A bed marks the beginning and end of the day, and can offer respite in the middle. It comforts us when we are least in control.

ABOVE A four-poster can anchor a room. The darkness of the "Re" bed by Christian Liaigre and its accompanying "Muse" bedside table helps to activate a geometry in the room. The bed area seems contained and has an Asian quality. The four-poster began to take shape in the fourteenth century—at first not with four posts, but a headboard and two footposts.

BELOW Khaki-green leather headboards with an urbane quality lift the plump twin beds of this guest bedroom out of the ordinary, making them part of the continuing design ethos that flows through the apartment.

BELOW The Villevoyes' bedroom is a multipurpose room, with a movie screen the width of the bed that springs out of a wooden chest. Another compartment at the end of the bed contains the projector, which peeps through a discreet hole.

ABOVE The master bedroom of the Zucker residence reiterates the yin-yang play of the house. The dark, oversized headboard, white walls, and traditional dark wood with ultra-modern aluminum contrast attractively. A bed without a surround in this vast space might look a little paltry. The egg is a lamp.

ABOVE An antique bed need not appear rustic and unglamorous: my own preference is for wrought-iron bedsteads, as opposed to the typical Victorian brass version. The focus of this bedroom is the bed, with its poetic beauty and sinuous lines, its head in complete symmetry with its foot.

FABRIC

ABOVE Rich luxury combines with demure simplicity in a chair from Donghia. Plain and textured-weave single-color fabrics must be durable. Wool and wool blends are upholstery classics. Cashmere's draping qualities and ultrasoft texture make it good for pillows or curtaining, but too fragile for upholstery. Light affects all fabrics and brings neutral, self-patterned, single colors to life. Weaves such as ridges and dotted textures are best seen under angled light.

OPPOSITE Patterns can be glorious: color, texture, and motifs add character to a room, especially if bold in design. Plants have always inspired fabric patterns; up to the seventeenth century, most floral designs were stylized rather than accurate pictures. The nineteenth century saw the rise of power looms and dyes that produced vivid colors, vastly increasing the scope for creativity. Pictorals (such as *toile de Jouy*), floral fabrics (preferably stylized) and geometric tapestries (top right)—these are hand-loomed in France—add a wealth of possibilities, but are best as accents. Pillows and throws are the answer, mixing eras and motifs. Fabrics inspired by North Africa and the East can be exotic and rich (top left). Straw, jute, and other natural fibers are delightful in summer (bottom left), and velvet can be versatile (bottom right), a lush background for glossy borders.

Modern fabrics may be produced from man-made or natural fibers, or a combination of the two: one is not necessarily better than the other. What the cloth is used for, however, should determine the choice of fabric, or fiber, before you think about patterned or solid.

What amounts to fabric snobbery means that designers have a difficult time persuading clients of the virtues of synthetic fibers. These are easy to care for, and top fabric companies J. Robert Scott, Larsen, Ulf Moritz, and Nya Nordiska, although working with natural fibers, too, create their most revolutionary designs using synthetics. Rayon and viscose, unlike true synthetics, are derived from the same cellulose polymers as cotton, hemp, and flax. Viscose readily absorbs water and loses strength when wet or if exposed to sunlight for long periods (although, like rayon, it does not fade), but it can be worked to resemble wool, silk, or other fabrics, and its moisture retention makes it comfortable next to skin.

Some natural fabrics, such as linen, conduct heat well and are appropriate for use in warm climates or during summer. Linen always feels cool to the touch and, used as table or bed linen, is usually white or pale and plain. Try to avoid "pastels," those pallid and diluted apologies for color. Solid-colored and self-patterned linens and silks (cotton-lined to prevent fading) are perfect at windows to keep out hot sun. Generally, solid fabrics are not appropriate for seating or cushion covers in hot climates, however, since dampness may cause staining, and water-marking is more evident on plain fabrics—in hot climates, designers

usually favor patterned pillow covers, whether linen, cotton, or silk. Sophisticated designers use other natural fibers, such as jute and hemp, too, to produce intricate weaves. The visual balance created by the use of solid-colored drapes, a bordered rug on a stone floor or a recessed plain rug within a wooden floor, and sofas, banquettes, and chairs accented with patterned cushions, is a sound and comfortable one.

Geometric patterns blend well in a classic interior. Many patterns are ancient: the Greek key pattern, for example, looks stunning as a border on upholstered furniture or on curtains. The Suzani patterns of North Africa and Asia travel well stylistically speaking, since their pattern is symmetrical and ordered, despite being based on curves.

Other traditional patterns can also work well. Tapestries and rich embroideries add texture as well as color, and warm up an otherwise "cool" interior. Although I am not a great fan of chintz, I have nothing against rose or other floral patterns if the motif is stylized. The rose is one of the most enduringly popular floral motifs for both woven and printed designs. My own preference is for medieval, Jacobean, and Arts and Crafts roses, which are wild, rather than the cultivated varieties found in Edwardian and Victorian designs.

In general, sweeps of solid fabric take the eye from plane to plane: a pattern will always distract the eye. Patterned fabric can be delightful as an accent or a bold statement, as in architect Michael Wolfson's bedroom (*see* page 176), where every wall is fabric-paneled in black *toile de Jouy* as a backdrop to modern cerused-oak furniture.

CURTAINS, SHADES, AND BLINDS

Curtains were originally intended to keep drafts out and warmth in, but today they serve many purposes. Shades are an alternative, altering the flow of light into a space as well as providing privacy.

Almost without exception, curtains are made from fabric. I say "almost" having observed an ingenious window treatment in Sally Sirkin Lewis's Beverly Hills home (*see* page 122), where strings of bathroom chain (the kind that attaches plugs to basins) hang from window-top to floor like a waterfall. This curtain of small metal beads complements Lewis's dramatic art and sculpture and perfectly suits the window walls

leading out to the courtyard garden. The chains whiz aside with ease (and make a lovely noise) for access to the yard, leaving the entire window wall naked. Fabric curtains would complicate the windows, and shades would be visible at the top, ruining the concept of a wall that isn't there.

The choice between curtains and shades depends on the use and role of the window. There is no point in adding curtains to a contemporary house if the architecture is pure, streamlined, and depends upon its indoor/outdoor aspect (*see* pages 32–33). But since many contemporary houses are south-facing in the northern hemisphere

or north-facing in the southern, protection is needed from sunlight so colors do not fade nor fabrics weaken, and privacy is also a consideration. Hence a home usually needs some sort of window treatment. Sliding doors benefit from shades or blinds, since they may lack wall space for curtains.

The play of light of a Venetian blind in a low-ceilinged, simply decorated room adds great charm. Shades can be made from almost any material and take various forms. Roman shades of continuous sheer fabric avoid the slat gaps of Venetian blinds, and allow in a delicate uniform light, as do rice-paper panels, a Japanese device.

LEFT The simple ring-and-pole method can make a curtain glide easily and help tailor a room, as long as rings and poles are metal and surface-treated. Here, the curtains are sewn puckered, maximizing the fabric's fullness, with the rings at the very top. The ceiling-mounted pole has more strength and looks neat on a ceiling-height window.

OPPOSITE, TOP LEFT Metal ring-and-pole systems glide much more smoothly than wooden ones (which are visually somewhat bohemian, and tend to jam, so drawing them by hand means a risk of damage to the fabric). Here, heavy white linen curtains are bordered in classic gray.

OPPOSITE, TOP RIGHT Unlined silk devoré will not keep warmth in, nor provide much privacy, but these issues may not matter—here, the window looks onto a private garden and full focus can be given to the delicious drapes, shaped by ornamental wall-secured tiebacks. Floaty fabrics demand great width. Depending on the type of heading and fabric, all curtains should be at least twice, if not three times, the width of the track length.

OPPOSITE, BOTTOM LEFT Airy linen curtains can look crisp, especially if the rod is substantial—these were made from long linen sheets from a convent. The forged iron rod has been custom-designed to harmonize with the shape of the window, and is a beautiful object in itself.

OPPOSITE, BOTTOM RIGHT Slub silk in a neutral color cascades to the floor. These curtains are black-silk-lined to block out light in a bedroom that doubles as a movie-viewing room: linings can insulate against cold, noise, or light. The tiebacks hold the curtains at floor level, an interesting variant of the usual waist-height version.

Curtains can only be used if the window permits. Sash windows can be curtained, as can windows that open outward; otherwise, shutters are the answer. It is not practical, nor elegant, to have to tuck curtains behind windows that open inward the French way. Patterned curtains are more costly than solid ones, since more fabric is needed to match the pattern at seams. (In a chic home, scraps should not be used to accessorize the same room: the effect would be too "matchy.") Curtains should glide with ease. If they are drawn by hand, the rings and rod must be unimpeded; thin drawing rods connected to curtaintops also ease movement.

Tiebacks are essential if curtains are voluminous—like a belt around an oversized coat. Curtains should usually reach the floor: there is nothing elegant about drapes flying at half mast, especially if radiators are visible beneath. The exceptions are those on small, high windows, and café curtains, which cover the lower half of a window and are effective in a kitchen niche or conservatory, allowing daylight in, but providing privacy. Blinds that extend up instead of down work well for the same reason. In the Bray-Schaible apartment (see pages 12–13), a shade of this kind emphasizes the fact that the furniture is all below waist height.

RIGHT AND FAR RIGHT There is nothing worse than shutting out sunlight by closing curtains, unless these are sheer—mull or linen, perhaps—and intended to filter light, making it more appealing and lengthening the life of furniture. Stylish curtains are often not only lined with sateen or silk, but also interlined with flannel, producing opulent folds and preventing light from seeping through at night. Used with formal curtains, blinds such as these thin nineteenth-century Japanese canes, cut, seamed, and trimmed with antique obi silk, are practical and luxurious.

RIGHT, BELOW Where refined masterpieces are made of wood and rustic materials, the setting must not be over- or under-played. Here, with George Nakashima sofas holding court, voluminous curtains would never work, and shades might be too clinical. The ceiling-to-floor outer curtains are mercerized silk, the wafts of inner curtain sheer linen. Textures and lines follow the tenor of the furniture.

BELOW These chains make a glorious swishing sound when drawn. Strands of ball-and-socket chain attached to tracks at the ceiling offer shade from harsh light, although some daylight seeps through. Reminiscent of chainmail (which should be more prevalent in couture), it makes a refreshing alternative to fabric, and is appropriate in a house that is effectively a gallery for powerful art.

ABOVE A ground-floor apartment in an Edwardian house on the corner of a London street suffers from the constant peering in of passersby. Ingeniously devised double-faced cotton window flaps (something I have not seen before) offer the perfect and simplest high-impact solution. Hooks on each side of window secure decorative rings sewn onto the fabric at half-height, so light can pour in above during the day. At night, the flaps are unfolded and the rings are hooked at ceiling height.

UPHOLSTERY

The key factor in upholstery is fabric durability. An apparel-quality silk devoré would disintegrate in days. Wool and its blends, on the other hand, are comfortable and durable, and need not look bulky.

Upholstery fabric alone can make the difference between a traditional classic and a new classic interior. Old classics that update effectively are plain, heavy mohair velvet, silk velvet, strie velvet, and corduroy. All highly textured, they go well with felts, linens, cottons, and other mixes. A new classic interior is marked by inclusion of very different fabrics, some inspired by men's suiting—herringbone, gabardine, pin-, and chalk stripes.

Buttonbacks can be good for securing fabric and creating a comfortably firm back. Jonathan Reed adapts the concept to great effect, with string knots on bench seats of putty-colored wool felt.

Tassels and braids, used long ago to disguise poorly finished seams and edges, are no longer necessary except for decoration. I would rather see magnificent, sculptural zoomorphic feet on upholstered furniture than decorative trimmings. But some people use tassels well, even in raffia, straw, or leather. Maureen Paley has added a sky-blue fringe to her Venetian-red velvet sofa, tipping her living room into the realm of the surreal.

ABOVE Cotton jumbo-wale corduroy is informal on the banquette and as a covering for the padded wall of the surrounding niche; it plays its part in a contrast of texture and color with the shiny woods and suede of this cozy antechamber to a bedroom. Corduroy, whether for clothes or for interiors, is always an intentional "dressing down"—which, as a concept, can be markedly chic.

OPPOSITE

TOP LEFT Jenny Armit's interiors are marked by her extraordinary color sense and attention to luxurious comfort. Magenta velvets rule this living room, while in the dining room behind, yellow velvet button-back chairs encircle a table. I believe in neatly tailored chairs and sofas; bulk and capaciousness are not necessarily hospitable.

TOP CENTER Upholstery must not be too padded. "It's as comfortable to sit in more understuffed furniture and easier to get in and out of it gracefully, as anyone knows who has watched a plump woman disengaging herself from the clutches of a low, deep and enveloping overstuffed chair," said Michael Greer in 1962.

TOP RIGHT In the aftermath of World War II, rationing restrictions meant that women in many countries had to be creative with clothing fabric: some wore parachute-silk slips, others paper dresses, and the truly canny made dresses from rose-adorned drapery and ended up camouflaged in their own homes. The use in the home of cloth designed for apparel did not become the vogue until much later, in the 1980s, when Ralph Lauren put pin- and chalk-stripes on chairs. Personally, I love the idea. Curtains made the female figure bulbous, but suit fabric can only trim the lines of a chair.

BOTTOM LEFT According to English decorating doyenne Nina Campbell, it is better to mix large pattern with small than use two medium-sized patterns. Jenny Armit, an Englishwoman now based in Los Angeles, agrees, as seen in this conservatory. The custom-designed carpet by Christine Van Der Hurd is geometric in pattern but on a large scale, superb grounding for the thinly striped pillows and upholstery. The delightful hexagonal stool, with its pert satin cushion, is enough to make me disagree with the American naturalist Henry David Thoreau, who wrote, "I would rather sit on a pumpkin and have it all to myself, than be crowded on a velvet cushion."

CENTER RIGHT Upholstered furniture must be finished at the edges, with gimp, piping, nailheads, or single self-weft. Gimp is a trimming made for upholstery (whereas galloon can be used on drapery, pillows, lampshades, and fabric-covered walls as well as upholstery). Piping is lovely on velvet.

BOTTOM RIGHT Judicious contrasts in texture and color are important in a town style. It can work very well to cover two out of three elements in related fabrics, or relate them through color or texture. On another note, beware of perching on edges of upholstered chairs, however politely: this will generally damage the internal structure.

DETAIL

ABOVE This claw-and-ball foot supports an unusual porcelain washbasin. In ancient Greece and Rome, furniture legs occasionally imitated those of animals or birds with hooves or claw feet. The *diphros*, a stool on four turned legs, was a Roman invention, often made of bronze, with curved legs ornamented with scrolls. Since ancient times, ornate feet have been intrinsic to classical—and therefore neoclassical—furniture.

OPPOSITE When people comment on the elegance of hands, they are admiring the beauty of the joints as much as the length of the fingers. Similarly with furniture, practical details need not be hidden, but can contribute to its attractiveness. This Danish 1960s table, in rosewood with stainless-steel legs, is more beautiful thanks to its joint, a type known as "through dovetail," in this case square cut. Typical joints used in furniture manufacture are "plain butt" and "tongue and groove" (both chiefly used in glued panels). The unseen joints of upholstered furniture are mostly simpler slot-in or peg-in methods. "Miter and spline," where two faces meet at 45 degrees like a picture frame, and "dovetail," seen here, are used primarily for internal box-type constructions.

Bric-a-brac, baubles, bangles, and beads do not constitute "details" in a sound classic interior: details are not frou-frou additions to a scheme, but integral to it. The shadow gaps between ceiling and wall and floor and wall in Terry Hunziker's home (*see* pages 46–47) are important architectural details. Not only do the recesses allow the walls to appear as if they are floating, they also prevent cracks from extending into the main body of the wall.

Architraves, baseboards, and molding were originally applied to walls for the same reason: to conceal potential cracks or, in the case of beading on doors, joints. Prior to the mid-eighteenth century, building construction required internal pilasters, corbels, and moldings to play a structural as well as a decorative role, so moldings were substantial, made of wood and stone. From the mid-eighteenth century on, the structural importance of moldings diminished. Plaster and papier-mâché were used, and neoclassical moldings became more discreet, flatter in profile, and more delicate in appearance. Recently, silicones and other flexible materials have reduced cracking, so moldings are no longer necessary as such.

Joints can be appealing as a decorative and functional detail. Old-fashioned wooden butterfly and dovetail joints—holding together pieces of wood or metal-wood combinations—are quite beautiful and, whether with a diagonal or square cut, secure well.

Whether disguising or elaborating a junction between adjacent surfaces, the simplest moldings are rectilinear, derived from the classical Greek and Roman orders, and shaped in profile into a variety of curved or angular forms. Elaborate moldings are often made up of the repeated shapes of ordinary decorative objects: coin, ribbon and rosette, bead and reel, and so on. Then there are moldings consisting of floral, mythological, or human forms such as acanthus leaves, sphinxes, griffins, and satyrs. Simple moldings can be highly appealing in the right circumstances, particularly if they form part of the architect's original plan, and occasionally if a room permits the later addition of such embellishment.

Beyond architectural detail, however, we must also look at the form of every element in a room, no matter how small and insignificant. Lamps, wastepaper baskets, candlesticks, and so on are necessary to our existence and must be scrutinized. How many times does a photographer have to avoid an interior shot of an entire wall because the electrical sockets are ugly or the lamp cords too fat and plastic?

One man who understands detail is British furniture designer David Linley. In *Design and Detail in the Home*, Linley pays tribute to his father, who trained as an architect and helped his son spot the finer elements of a home: "We were taught to really look: at architecture, at rooms, at furniture and paintings, and also at the smaller details that help make an interior—the locks on a door, the legs on a piece of furniture, even the light switches. Thus, whether confronted by an eighteenth-century cabinet or a tubular steel chair, we learned to appreciate the quality of its craftsmanship and attention to detail."

LIGHTS

Decorative objects such as lights are the first elements to date. The only guidelines can be careful selection, insight, and a certain amount of historical knowledge.

Some craftspeople do achieve timelessness with lamp design: Serge Roche (who worked in plaster), Diego Giacometti (who used wrought iron), and master *ferronier* Gilbert Poillerat produced exquisite lamps and sconces nearly three-quarters of a century ago, copies of which are now made for today's glamorous venues. London chef-restaurateur Marco Pierre White mixes originals with lamps "inspired by" the geniuses above, to superb effect.

A lamp must not only provide the right light (*see* pages 60–65), but also be dainty enough not to upset a room's balance. Wide table-lamp bases are anathema to me, and spherical ones with flat coolie-hat lampshades look squat and take up table space. Desk lamps are another animal: many commercial designs are streamlined and effective.

Lamp shades add glamour as long as they do not become the focal point of a room. The lights designed by Patrice Butler, with shades by milliner Philip Treacy, are some of the most stupendous—a hat shape adorning a base made of rich materials such as hand-blown glass, wrought iron, or crystal.

Lusters, sconces, and freestanding fixtures with no illumination source, whose crystals glisten when light hits, may evoke Victoriana but can be lovely nonetheless. There are custom-made contemporary versions with a play of light that is magical.

ABOVE "The Servant's candlesticks are generally broken, for nothing lasts forever. But you may find out expedients; you may conveniently stick your candle in a bottle... or upon its own grease upon a table... or you may cut a hole in a loaf and and stick it in there," wrote Jonathan Swift in 1745. A candle needs nothing more than a hole, and a lamp nothing more than a power supply, yet lamps can be designed to meet complex challenges, particularly given the scope of a large, loft-like space. These dangling spot lamps hanging from a ceiling track can be used for accent or en masse to create the illusion of a lower ceiling.

OPPOSITE

TOP LEFT In the seventeenth century, candle wall lights were elaborate indications of status, and sconces remain the simplest way to light a room. The backplate of this form is both old and new: old sconces supported a backplate with a ledge or holder for the candle.

TOP CENTER This spherical lamp by Aublet is highly tactile. The base is perfectly balanced and rotates in its cradle with just the right resistance so it does not slip when positioned. Its head tilts at your whim. Not only can light be directed accurately; the body of the lamp is pure sculpture.

TOP RIGHT Even today, the French rarely use ceiling lights, except grand chandeliers, and the sconce has not once been out of fashion in Paris. Nye Basham's sconces, from the early to mid twentieth century, look as if they once lit an ocean liner's restaurant or a theater.

LEFT To supplement her lighting, Holly Hunt has floor lamps with flexible stems so that the shades bend at a touch. "People don't pay enough attention to lighting," she says. "They spend a lot of time working out details, finding the right pillows, then stick a halogen light in and call it done."

CENTER One of a pair of French metal lamps from the 1970s, probably designed for a living room, brings a touch of modernity to this bedroom, as well as illuminating its surroundings.

RIGHT This lamp with wooden base and steel shade is Italian 1950s by Arteluce. Its unusual form is perfectly complemented by the leather-seated ladderback chair (one of a set), which is country Georgian, circa 1790.

BOTTOM LEFT Just as *haute couture* becomes ready-to-wear and then department stores bring out their own version, chain stores now carry well-designed lamps. There should be no fear of adding an inexpensive new lamp if it seems to do the job.

BOTTOM CENTER Many lampshades are too opaque, blocking out light or redirecting it. Just as legs look better in sheer hose than in two-dimensional opaque, so with this shade: a second skin of darker fabric is loosely puckered over stretched skin behind; light is emitted through both.

BOTTOM RIGHT A spiral-seashell-inspired patinated cast-brass table lamp, designed by Paul Verburg originally for London's Oak Room, has the added detail of an antique-style gold-silk braided cord. The design was carved into wood, which was then used as a mold for sandcasting.

DOOR HARDWARE

In the quest for harmonious order, not a stone—or door handle—can be left unturned. Door furniture can be interesting and contribute decoratively to a room. Some is pure art and sells as such, for example, handle designs by Diego Giacometti and Antoni Gaudí. Others are minimal, in an attempt to be seamless. Above all, handles (generally lever locks) and knobs must anchor securely: wobbly ones irritate, make a terrible racket, and can ruin a finish. The mechanism must glide as easily as a monkey on a greased pole.

Many wooden doors traditionally had fingerplates, to protect the surface and improve appearance. These are now unfashionable, although escutcheons, which protect the wood around a keyhole, remain popular.

Metal is a favorite for door hardware, since the mechanisms are metal. It is hard-wearing and matches the hinges, which, if exposed, must also be stylish. Resin composites, warm to the touch, and bone can be attractive, but may date a room. Bakelite, for instance, looks very 1930s. Porcelain is delightful on some cabinets, but looks "country cottage" on doors.

The form of a handle is important. A knob must be easy on the fingers, a handle the right size for an adult hand.

RIGHT A tiny finger-sized door pull by Antoni Gaudí is the ultimate icing on the cake, decorative but diminutive, and I would put these everywhere. The small handle is beautifully formed and sensuous to the touch, and here serves to pull an entire closet out of the wall.

LEFT Stylish door hinges may be plated in chrome, nickel, gold, or silver; or cast, wrought, or forged iron. Hinges come in different configurations according to function: straight butt hinges are the most common. These heavy-duty but attractive brass swivel hinges are appropriate for French doors, double-opening doors, or any door that folds back flat against the wall or its partner.

LEFT, BELOW Lever handles, especially heavy ones, as here, contain a spring to bring the lever up to the correct level. These patinated bronze handles are sand-cast ("lost wax" is another method used). A custom-made handle requires individual calculation, since its weight dictates the strength of spring needed to keep it from sagging.

OPPOSITE, TOP LEFT To reduce their weight, lever handles can be hollow or, as here, contain cutouts in the patinated metal. Custom-made handles, which can also be made from bronze-filled resin (with a metal-effect finish that can be patinated), are high-quality pieces—jewelry for the door.

OPPOSITE, TOP CENTER William and Mary door rings in bronze, here reproduced as a custom design (with a square attachment rather than round, and on a larger scale), open the doors of a vellum cabinet. Some methods of metalworking remain unaltered since biblical times.

OPPOSITE, TOP RIGHT Custom-made handles may suit important doors or cabinets, but there is no need to make the financial leap of using them for all doors. Sleek off-the-shelf alternatives include handles made of plastics, transparent Lucite being possibly the most attractive.

OPPOSITE, LEFT Interior, non-locking doors do not need escutcheons, and are all the better for it. This solid bronze lever handle by Antoni Gaudí is even more sinuous and pure, thanks to the fact that the plate behind the handle clips over the fixing plate, with no screws visible.

OPPOSITE, CENTER A stainless-steel recessed handle on a sliding door lifts and turns 90 degrees to open or close the door. The visual effect is neat, and the mechanism smooth. In selecting handles with complicated mechanisms, be sure they are high-quality—a door can be pulled off its hinges.

OPPOSITE, RIGHT Lever handles work, of course, on a lever principle: a regular-length lever requires less than one-third of the force of a door knob to operate. This lever handle and its finger plate are one, the plate protecting the finish of the door, but neatly blending with the handle.

OPPOSITE, BOTTOM LEFT These handles are original to the house. Paltry knobs and handles will ruin a good door. Brass finishes can be lacquered to minimize tarnishing; if already tarnished, they can be cleaned in an acid bath. Rusted ironwork can be revived with caustic paint stripper.

OPPOSITE, BOTTOM CENTER This void, a slot, is the most honest and immaculate kind of door "handle" for a glass and metal sliding door, but is not suitable for all doors. Most designers will produce a manner of opening and closing a door that forms an intrinsic part of the door.

OPPOSITE, BOTTOM RIGHT Good door hardware lasts forever and gives distinction to a home; this exquisite antique brass knob enjoys the patina of time. With a lever inside, it can be turned gently to lock French doors.

ART AND ORNAMENT

ABOVE Some collectors are fanatics who will stop at nothing to fill their homes with all manner of paraphernalia, including marbles, "outsider" art, and weathervanes. These kinds of collections should be allocated entire rooms or at least drawers or sections of shelves, so that they can be viewed if and when guests are interested in exploring a subject perhaps not entirely dear to their heart. Small groupings of items linked by a common thread are a different matter and can make an appealing tabletop arrangement.

OPPOSITE An eclectic collection of ornaments can be perceived as a psychodrama, and entrance halls can provide gallery space in miniature. Hall tables and their accoutrements may offer an inkling of what is to come, in terms of decoration or the mindset of the inhabitant. In Ted Russell's hallway, eyes stare back at you from the Stefano Castrovona painting *Devoid No. 1*, in front of which stand Greek figures, silver and glass bowls, a porcelain pagoda-type tower, and an urn, all flanked by a pair of candlesticks. The combination of materials is rich and dynamic, and leans toward classicism.

When I was in my teens, my mother used to tell me that nuns have the best skin, because they have no mirrors. At the time my focus was on superficial matters, but in retrospect I think she was referring to inner beauty. Likewise, ornament in an interior should be of intrinsic, not surface, beauty.

I rather like one-liners, although I am often not sure if they are meant to elicit sympathy or shock. One I heard the other day (not from my mother, I hasten to add) was uttered by an unusually ugly-beautiful woman, who said: "I don't use make-up, I only use knives." Such an approach—go for fundamental meaning, not surface glamour—can be applied to interior design, especially pictures. I am thinking of "decorator art," as it is known, whereby pictures are created during or just after interior installations, to form part of the décor. Such degree of "make-up" cannot surely be sound (although that is not to say that rooms cannot be designed around pictures—*see* pages 44–45). What is needed are knives, palettes, oils, and canvas to create real pictures, purchased with commitment, that can move around the home and from house to house.

Pictures and mirrors can be hung in all manner of ways: as singular pieces central to a chest or above a fireplace mantel, in pairs side by side or one above another, or in what art expert Alec Cobbe described as a "rich hang," a European practice where collections of pictures are hung on chains and cover entire walls in libraries, halls, and drawing rooms. If pictures are hung at one level around a room, the guideline should be the occupant's eye level; any higher or lower, and the picture's apparent perspective will be altered.

Mathematical precision is the key to hanging pictures—so beware the room with no real right angles. Take a horizontal line, the most obvious being a mantelpiece, and work from this. Pictures with a uniform visual baseline have a stabilizing effect.

A fairly new way of displaying pictures and mirrors is on a sill or shelf. The pictures are largely free-standing, being slightly supported by the wall. This is an exciting development, since the variables are enormous and pictures can be moved around at whim. The uniform baseline also means they cannot go askew.

Art and ornaments do not have to be highly decorative or ornate. A vase may be a vessel or a sculpture, and a group of vases or pots can form a group sculpture if their forms, textures, and colors are harmonious. An object that stands alone is clearly venerated by its owner. I once picked up what seemed to be just a dimpled rock— a beautiful but plain object—that had pride of place in the home of painter Erez Yardini. To my surprise, it was more than five thousand years old. Some objects are collected for their value and historical significance, others for their intrinsic beauty. The thing about pots and some sculpture is that they are timeless in form, and their provenance and value cannot be predicted from their appearance.

PICTURES AND MIRRORS

Choosing paintings is a very personal thing, and one person's idea of abstract art, for example, may be different from another's. If you cannot have what you really want, create something yourself— but for goodness' sake, not as part of the decorative scheme. One of the most effective "works of art"— I use the term loosely—in our home is a 9-foot-by-5-foot (2.7-meter-by-1.5-meter) sepia photographic image printed on canvas. The combination of canvas and pixels gives the image grain and depth. It shows the opening of the Egyptian royal tombs in the 1920s, and was a snapshot taken by an onlooker: now, in a heavy mahogany frame, it is majestic, extending the width of the dining room's chimney frame. We also have collections of seventeenth- and eighteenth-century Italian prints and large pieces of colorful art and sculpture against painter's white in the living room. It helps having a sculptor for a husband— not that we keep many of his pieces for long. Although little of our furniture changes, the art and accessories do constantly.

Mirrors serve three purposes: as decorative objects, light reflectors, and devices for mirroring other surfaces, thus extending or altering the aspect of a room. Unlike pictures, mirrors can be designed specifically for a location.

ABOVE The art in Holly Hunt's dining room is mainly American gestural abstraction, although the forms are related to Picasso, Miró, and Matisse. An "Ubud" table with crazy leg detail and "Archipel" chairs by Christian Liaigre enhance the art through their graphic quality. Made from a single piece of lumber, the table had to be sawn in half to enter the apartment.

OPPOSITE

TOP LEFT The twentieth century saw the emergence of art with no overt connection with the physical world. Abstract art baffles people because it poses difficulties of judgment and understanding, and calls into question the nature of art, but it is a misconception to think of it as a mere design device. Sally Sirkin Lewis's collection includes #3 by John McLaughlin (oil on canvas, 1963), and Mel Kendrick's sculpture #2 (bronze with silver nitrate, 1986).

TOP RIGHT Nine metal cubes, purchased as installation art, have been pushed into the wall in a defined pattern but turned randomly, creating a set sculpture that gives the illusion of being kinetic. (A craze for this kind of art, purchased for one location and created directly on the wall, the owner of the art having the right to re-create it when moving location, was begun by British artist Damien Hirst.) Below the artwork, the chest makes a stunning contribution to both ornamentation and storage space.

BOTTOM LEFT Neoclassical pieces may seem somewhat conservative. But art is a very subjective thing, and I think any kind of art, valuable or "found," can work well, as long as the choice is based on passion.

BOTTOM RIGHT The advent of photography in the 1840s freed artists from the restrictions of realism. Much American art in the years after World War II featured black pigment, in a kind of exploration of the woes of war. From 1950, painters like Franz Kline began to paint white ground as thickly as black shapes, overlapping paint until the sections appeared locked together. He later used a wall painter's brush, delighting in scale.

SCULPTURE & CERAMICS

Classical statuary is not a prerequisite for a classic interior, but it is certainly popular. Extensive collections of artifacts were assembled in Rome by as early as the sixteenth century, but collecting classical antiquities did not become à la mode on an international scale until the late seventeenth century. This cultural treasure hunt, which began among esthetes and the elite, and expanded in the nineteenth century to include the affluent middle classes and "tourists," survives in the antiquarian's showroom today.

Sadly, demand for scraps of history eventually outstripped availability, and led to a glut of fakes. The most valued of these are neoclassical sculptures of figures and busts, produced in some quantity during the second half of the nineteenth century. Some are by an American, Hiram Powers. Unlike artists who preferred gods as models, Powers empathized with the anonymous of antiquity. His most sought-after pieces, then and now, are variations of the "Greek Slave." Most statues, columns and obelisks, pots and bowls from antiquity are safely tucked up in museums; the "classical" pieces in private collections are almost invariably these neoclassical copies.

When it comes to pottery, some people look to ancient pieces,

OPPOSITE

TOP LEFT In an apartment in a London garden square, a table top is a platform for monumental objects. Their scale means they would more usually be displayed as individual pieces rather than as a group, but the effect is truly stately. Some groupings are an invitation to pick things up and admire them—definitely not the case here.

TOP RIGHT The forms of animal parts have been emulated in furniture for thousands of years. Particularly in the twentieth century, human skeletal structure has also become a blueprint for furniture (the work of Antoni Gaudí, for example, under the Art Nouveau umbrella). The moose or elk head is less favored now that hunting is less popular, but skulls and bones can still make impressive and inexpensive sculptures.

RIGHT Anything can be art, depending on how it is presented and its *raison d'être*. The seasoned traveler might pick up a few pieces to send home as mementoes of an exotic trip—a wonderful way to introduce alternative elements such as tribal art into a room, especially if you have an idea of the culture behind the object.

BOTTOM LEFT Carefully placed objects include a rather lovely, ethereal nineteenth-century copy of a neoclassical head, a 1970s ashtray in horn and chrome, and a 1940s ceramic vase, which rather prosaically came from an office at EMI. Here products from different times and disparate origins blend together as a composite whole.

BOTTOM CENTER A bold classical embellishment: nineteenth-century copies of classical statuary make fabulous icons and the most acceptable nudes, perhaps because history distances us. Stylized or abstract nudes (Henry Moore and Fernando Botero) are generally acceptable, too, because their form is distanced from reality. Personally, I can live with all manner of nudes, no matter how explicit. Some can, some can't.

BOTTOM RIGHT Safe but select. In choosing sculpture to live with, whether valuable or just an object of desire, do not feel bound to go to extremes. Nor need you be a snob about materials: fiberglass and plastics can produce decent effigies, as can stone, plaster, and marble. Many replicas are effective. As a dramatic cloak suits an evening at the opera, so a dramatic sculpture or ornament requires guts. The gilded console is slate-topped.

ABOVE Some prefer to avoid obvious ornament in favor of art and sculpture, which is in itself ornamental. In the 1960s and '70s, continental Europe provided many colorful artists whose uplifting work did not appear entirely serious: the mechanized junk sculptures by Swiss artist Jean Tinguely come to mind. On the windowsill to the right of this room is a bronze sculpture by Lynn Chadwick; in the foreground is an early model of the *Titanic*.

especially from Japan and China, while others are drawn to modern work from around the world. Highly collectible modern ceramics include the works of Lucie Rie and Rupert Spira, who takes some of his inspiration from the surface scratches of pre-Columbian Mimbres pottery. These fine lines were "used as a texture, not a decoration," he explains, and were "integral to the pot." He sees such a pot as "a map of everything that has gone into it," he adds. "I am fascinated by the capacity of objects to reveal their origin and to express something intangible and yet intimate." Spira, among others, is not remotely interested in function, although the pots and bowls he makes are usable as containers. Their shapes are the currency of an art that can be thought of as abstract form, he feels, "the functionality only one aspect of its capacity and potency."

ABOVE Pots are not the same as vases. A vase is for cut flowers, and flowerpots for live plants with soil, but small pots serving as decoration are probably left best containing nothing at all. Some might have had a purpose originally—for oils or incense—but most contemporary pots are created as objects, not vessels. The second-most unattractive addition to a home, after dried flowers, is a pot containing potpourri, which can only become dusty potpourri over time. Potpourri has its place in closets, but then so does cedar wood, which not only has a pleasant aroma but also deters moths.

OPPOSITE

TOP LEFT Simple wood or iron candle holders were used in churches before the eleventh century. By the thirteenth century, coronas or hoops of metal hung from the ceiling, with spikes for candles or cups for oil ("chandelier" is from the French *chandelle*, meaning candle). Candlestick forms have changed little; these, by Calvin Klein, are silver. Candlelight is magic in a room, and candlesticks add glamour and romance.

TOP RIGHT There is something sublime about the delicacy of these silver flower vases by Elsa Peretti for Tiffany, meant for a single flower. A vase may be defined as a vessel whose height is great in proportion to its width. These vases, with impressed thumbprint design, have great elegance in proportion to their size.

BOTTOM LEFT The fluid form of this piece offsets the rectilinearity of the pale bleached-oak coffee table, made in four sections. The beauty of the ensemble, however, lies in the subtle contrast of textures—both slightly rough to the touch, the pot more bisquelike and crisp, the table more blunt—and the similarity of color. The form of this piece and its shadow reminds me of a sculptural hat.

BOTTOM RIGHT The world of ceramics is a fascinating one, with multiple textures. Porcelain is transparent, and has an audible ring when tapped; earthenware is opaque and more robust. Slips and glazes can take years to perfect, and become intrinsic to the pots. My favorite, in appearance and execution, is a pot burnished with the back of a spoon, then fired in an underground peat kiln. The finish is like dark pewter.

An entire kitchen wing has been added to
this building. Its front-to-back axis provides
ease of movement, a view, and access to the
terrace and yard. The dining room is
reached via doors on the opposing wall to
the stove and built-in entertainment center.
The workstation islands, black-stained
maple cabinets topped with 10-foot-long
(3-meter) counters of unseamed granite,
work well in a kitchen of such scale since
they give more work space than they would
if placed against walls; furniture in the
center of a room can increase workable
space and improve traffic flow. When not in
use, this hardly looks like a kitchen at all.

FUNCTION

The principles of architecture
and interior design are applied
differently according to the
function of a space. Some areas
are used primarily for activity or
occupations: tasks are to be
achieved, there is much
movement, and it is important
to facilitate productivity and
flow. Other spaces are dedicated
to repose, which is often what
follows on from ease of passage
or productivity. Then, of course,
there are rooms that combine
quiet restfulness with
recreational or other activities—
either simultaneously or at
different times of day.

ACTIVITY

Rooms of function are too often neglected in the grand scheme. All activity rooms—whether task venues or areas mainly used for through movement—are rooms of productivity, but as well as serving their function, they must adhere to the general aesthetic of the home. Circulation is a major issue: in these spaces there are numerous tasks to be done, many of which require tools, yet at the same time free and frequent movement around the space is necessary. In designing a kitchen, bathroom, or study particularly, many a potential pitfall must be negotiated, and intelligent location of storage and equipment is paramount. On a more subtle level, not only must lighting be correctly task-focused, but both lighting and color schemes should be enlivening and conducive to productivity without being overstimulating, and should lead people through the spaces in an appropriate manner (see pages 60–67 and 82–85).

Probably the greatest amount of through activity takes place in the hallway, but even here there is a choice of psychological approach. Having announced a spectacle to come, a hallway can function either as a passageway or as an activity center. The late Italian architect Renzo Mongiardino used the rhythm of a corridor's length, which is exaggerated by its narrowness, to shape the approach. If he was treating the space as a passageway, he would pursue a "theatrical-perspective effect," whereby repeated architectural elements culminated in a focal point at each end of the gallery, creating the illusion of a grand passage and enlivening adjacent rooms. If choosing to treat the hallway as an activity center, he would aim to concentrate the life of the household in the lengthy corridor, so that the space included everything required for activities such as reading, music, display, and conversation. Life streamed through the long gallery, and adjoining rooms became intimate refuges.

The dimensions of a hallway usually determine the treatment required to make it function to best effect. Mongiardino explained how to transform a long room: "Small vaults, reductions in height, divisions, pilaster strips, matching doors and openings to adjacent rooms, symmetries, panels or mirrors—all skillfully arranged—can transform an unfortunate corridor into a cheerful little gallery." In a square-shaped room, the walls, having the same dimensions, take on equal value, but a lengthy gallery lends itself to the use of perspective.

The design of activity rooms is not always predictable. A bathroom may cater for a guest dropping by—witness the daybed in Andrée Putman's Knokke-Le-Zoute interior (see page 152)—or for swimming as well as ablutions, as in the bathroom by Larry Booth (see pages 36–37), or be deemed a room for relaxation. A kitchen can be a niche or the hub of the home, used for activities from entertaining to watching television. A study may have to accommodate a posse of clients for a business meeting or be a homework refuge: like the hall, the study is in a sense a room of both repose and activity.

RIGHT "'There won't be any revolution in America,' said Isadore. Nikitin agreed. 'The people are all too clean. They spend all their time changing their shirts and washing themselves. You can't feel fierce and revolutionary in a bathroom.'" Whatever the reason, the prediction, from *Juan in America* by Scottish novelist Eric Linklater (1899–1974), proved thankfully correct. A room of activity has to be appropriate to the activity to be performed in it, and little more.

HALLS & STAIRS

Just as the courtyard serves as an overture to the Italian palazzo and the French *hôtel particulier*, the hallway is a fanfare for the common man, the place that announces a home to guests and where they themselves are announced. "I don't like being hurled into someone's living room: it's so absolutely American to open the front door and find oneself right in the middle of a conversation," says Missouri-born interior designer John F. Saladino, noted for his refined, simple, and livable interiors. The central hall in his own home has arched corridors leading in four directions. "Having parents of European origin brought a lot to bear on my sensibilities," he says. "It's very important to concern ourselves with the negative spaces and not

ABOVE LEFT Stephen Sills and James Huniford made the three original rooms of the second floor of this house into one, with the central section forming the mouth of a staircase that sweeps down to the first floor and front door, and up to bedroom suites and an office. Substantial yet elegant, the entire stairwell was redesigned from scratch to give proportionate importance to the staircase and the rooms to which it delivers people.

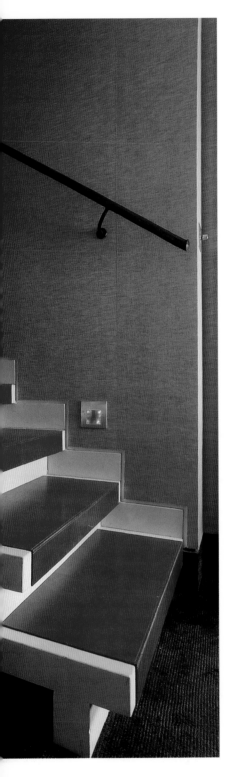

LEFT Some staircases are meant to blend into the background and be purely functional; others are not. It is difficult to walk past this system, in limestone with tan leather stair treads, without stopping in awe at its attention to detail and masculine beauty. All elements in Jonathan Reed's schemes are custom-made, so every part is fit for the job and high on aesthetics. Here, in an interior for a London client, the handrail is forged steel.

BELOW The tiny front hall of this small row house leads to the only slightly wider rear hallway, on a lower level, seen here. This part of the house has been converted to include a bathroom, above which are the kitchen and dining room. The door on the left opens into a walled garden. A French nineteenth-century gilt mirror with grapevine and floral motifs makes the small space seem larger. The patinated bronze lamp is by Paul Verburg.

only what we put in a room, because it is not just a receptacle that you stuff with furnishings or people."

I agree with Saladino that a room should not be a receptacle, certainly not if it is a circulation space. A row of chairs in a long hall or entrance foyer is uninviting, as if you are waiting to be seen. If chairs and tables are dotted around the perimeter of a relatively square hallway, the furniture will rarely be used and the space will look like a home for the elderly. Sensitive groupings, so that people can converse, are better.

Hall tables were originally intended for calling cards and letters; later came the telephone table. Since most telephones today are portable, we rarely have use for for such tables and their solitary chair. Few

regret their demise—they are no loss aesthetically, and in most homes the hall is an impossible place for intimate telephone conversations.

The grandest fanfare of all is a descent from a splendidly crafted staircase of substantial width. The staircase has long had a powerful hold on the imagination. It is a key element of architecture, a status that derives as much from its symbolic and aesthetic power as from its functionality.

According to traditional etiquette, there are four situations (feminism aside) in which a man should "precede a lady": when entering a restaurant or venue where he has made a reservation; when alighting from a train (often awkwardly high); when stepping onto a boat (in inappropriate footwear, perhaps); and when descending a staircase less than four feet wide. A narrow staircase, after all, may be rickety or lack a handrail, and he might be needed to break her fall. In a classic interior, of course, there will be no such problems. Too grand a staircase, on the other hand, can become a whirlpool that swallows up everything around it—think of *Gone with the Wind*.

If a workably grand entrance is the aim, Saladino has the knack. Borrowing architectural features from antiquity to

LEFT In Terry Hunziker's multifaceted duplex in a circa 1898 former hotel, where "surfaces provide the interest," the hall is defined by a steel runner recessed into the floor. A rust-colored floating wall helps separate the stairs from the gallery, adds another surface for furniture and art, and serves to direct the flow of movement (it can be walked around entirely). The circular painting, which insinuates circular motion, is a 1992 oil by Ken Kelly.

augment dimensions, and adding a few pieces of functional furniture, he has always been able to make a diminutive hall seem imposing. He might include a hall table or an urn, bringing the outside in and emphasizing the hall as a transition zone between garden and home. He creates charming smaller enclaves using tricks of color and artistry in the tradition of Mongiardino, who would place a collection of Palissy ceramics in a narrow corridor so that they caught the light from a window. Individual pieces of bold art do not always work in a hall or passageway, however, since they can be too imposing and stop passersby in their tracks, and their scale may be wrong for the space.

Staircases in evidence in a hall suggest potential fluidity of movement to other levels (*see* page 144). In some formal European houses, particularly the more Germanic, the hallway or corridor is presented as a solitary entity: the stairs are usually utterly unimposing, hidden behind doors that avoid grandeur (*see* page 103). The focus is thus on connections to rooms, and activity appears contained floor by floor. Far from diminishing the dramatic impact, this opens the possibility of making a new entrance on each floor.

ABOVE Keith Day and Peter Sheppard modeled this hall in an upper-floor apartment in London on a Venetian street, hence the lack of baseboard. The doors are painted to resemble exterior doors, and walls are color-washed to resemble stone. Based on a pavement in front of the Church of San Giorgio Maggiore in Venice, the floor is painted wood, adorned with eighteenth-century stone columns at the front and seventeenth-century oak columns (originally at Battersea House hospital) at the rear. The boar resting on an oak beam in the foreground is Indian. The hallway stairs replace a bathroom and are painted to look like stone.

RIGHT After two years of major renovations, the Collett-Zarzycki partnership, who describe their work as "considered," turned five apartments, in a heritage building with roots in the 1860s, into one house. The staircase had to be resited, literally sidelined: shifted from its dominant central position where it obstructed both the light and the view. Now the rooms facing the garden flow freely and are divided only on purpose. The glass finial is a quartz crystal sphere, and the Chinese cabinets are old (not custom-made as the fit would suggest). The walls are covered in stained white plaster, and the floors are York stone.

KITCHENS

In the 1950s, economic growth in the United States and Europe led to a housing boom and the production of a whole range of goods made from new materials, ownership of which was perceived to be indicative of a new, more affluent lifestyle. Following the poverty of the Depression in the late 1920s and '30s and the disruption of war in the 1940s, Americans had smaller families and embraced consumerism. Furniture design took advantage of new technology and materials, and the influence of good design became evident in mass-produced and utilitarian goods, as it is today. The built-in kitchen became the housewife's "workstation."

The key to a successful kitchen is the integration of classic elements and modern equipment. The kitchen is one area where old can mix with new and new with new,

ABOVE LEFT Robust materials are utilized on the lower cabinets, more perishable (pewter and silver-leaf decoration) on the upper. This kitchen is the hub of the house, and its well-planned interior reflects its constant use and its owners' love of entertaining and good food. The forged-steel medieval-inspired chandelier and the stools were designed by Collett-Zarzycki.

ABOVE The dining "niche" in a Belgian apartment by Andrée Putman contains the most basic but functional of dining rooms. Even the table (on wheels) could vanish. The niche acts as a walk-through to kitchen and entry hall, but can be partitioned off by folding and sliding screens.

ABOVE RIGHT Kitchen design is rarely effortless. Zarzycki's own kitchen has been built in light European oak: the "whiskey-oak" floor has been created from old oak distillery vats, cut down to size, then planed for use as flooring. The countertops are dark "Pietro San Marco" limestone. The rectangular ceiling lamp echoes the central table, which also acts as a work surface.

ABOVE FAR RIGHT In what appears a closet, this minute kitchen emits simplicity, but is highly considered. The three cabinets above the only work surface are placed with mathematical precision. Gaps between them make the kitchen seem larger and taller, leading the eye vertically.

as long as the materials used are uncompromising in quality and durability. In general, kitchen materials mix well, aesthetically speaking, partly because there are relatively few materials suitable for kitchen use. Stainless steel always looks stylish and complements modern appliances. It is possible to incorporate refined elements, as witnessed in the townhouse in London's Notting Hill designed by Collett-Zarzycki (*see* above left), where silver and pewter leaf adorn upper cabinet doors.

Black or white marble, Corian (a new, dense composite material), and the less expensive, beautiful but rather nastily named Millennium (another composite) make durable and luxurious countertop surfaces. The density of marble means it lags behind the ambient temperature so remains cool and is useful in warm conditions. Other advantages of these materials are that they can support chopping, are easily washed down, and give the impression of cleanliness.

Tiles are good on floors—ceramic tiles or quarry tiles—and, stylistically, the one room in the house that can take terracotta tiles is the kitchen. Once down, they should be kept waxed to produce and sustain a patina. If tiles are used on countertops, the grouting can be difficult to keep clean and their "bittiness" can be

To smarten up a wayward nineteenth-century room, where right angles are questionable and character is the watchword, Maureen Paley commissioned a kitchen to fit her space from an industrial company, preferring to have control over the final image and not buy off the shelf. The kitchen is successful because Paley has a good eye and understands function. The steel surrounds an old porcelain sink.

RIGHT The breakfast bar is somewhat of an anathema in Europe, but still very popular in the United States and the southern hemisphere—New Zealand and South Africa, for example, where there is great potential for building from scratch. More because of lack of space than eating habits, in Europe it is mostly just not feasible to consider allowing space for a breakfast bar: architects are employed to renovate, restore, and reorganize existing spaces rather than build new ones.

RIGHT A 1970s-designed built-in kitchen which, in its day, showed the highest quality and good forethought (the burners are separate from the oven, which is at waist height—not generally seen until well into the twentieth century—and there is a powerful extractor fan above). Architect Michael Wolfson decided to retain the kitchen, not remove it, although it is not original to the apartment on the top floor of a nineteenth-century building. Now as then, the kitchen functions adequately. Good design does last.

RIGHT The first built-in kitchens appeared in the United States in the years after World War II, when the country led the world in the field of domestic gadgetry. During the 1950s it became recognized that the kitchen was not so much a place for domestic drudgery as the household equivalent of a laboratory or workshop. This sterilization of the kitchen scene was necessary for technology to progress and be housed. Perhaps today we can put the humanity back into the kitchen and find a happy medium.

unattractive and distracting. Metro tiles—elongated rectangular ceramic tiles, generally in white—can, however, be attractive on walls. But ornate mosaics, to my mind, should be left in Morocco or ancient Rome: as a decorative element, they do not travel well.

In a small kitchen, the use of one material throughout lends coherence to a space that can do with a minimum of distraction. Avoid an entirely wooden kitchen, however, unless it is light-colored, because it will be difficult to light adequately. Larger kitchens can take more diverse materials and may end up looking very painterly if, say, planes of stainless steel meet planes of marble and wood. Kitchens that form part of an open-plan, no matter what size, should include limited materials so that the fluidity of the space is not broken up visually.

The basic elements of a kitchen are a sink and its surround, countertop, refrigerator, and stove. The next-most important are storage, and a table and chairs or bar stools, if the kitchen is also to function as an eatery. Everything else is superfluous to requirements. We have no modern conveniences in our kitchen apart from a dishwasher, a cappuccino "whizzer," as we call it, and a garbage disposal. If you are fond of kitchen utensils and accouterments, make sure you have adequate storage space and work surfaces. Personally, I think a countertop, like a desk, should be clear at the end of the day.

Our kitchen is a decent size, but I dream of a bigger kitchen still, whose center would be a large rectangular island of stainless steel with a sink, a prep area, and somewhere to sit and eat. All appliances would be contained within this island, and the walls would be empty save for art. The workstation is back, it seems, although I would prefer not to be chained to it.

ABOVE LEFT What more does one need? Overlooking the upper terrace and a panoramic skyline of downtown Seattle, Terry Hunziker's bathroom is monastic but a room with a view—of 1920s and '60s office buildings and '80s and '90s skyscrapers. Japanese maples and white hydrangeas fill Chinese pots on the terrace immediately outside; the door to the terrace is kept open all summer long.

LEFT In this bleached teak-clad bathroom, the daybed is meant for lounging on after the bath, or for a chat if a friend drops by. The white bath, in volcanic rock, sits centrally in the room and overlooks the rear terrace. Recessed lit floor panels between the marble and the wood of the floor help "elevate" the bath (so that it is as if on a stage). To either side of the day bed, enormous boxed closets are disguised as regular doors: handles pull the closets forward into the room. A close-up mirror (as on the blue shelf, *see also* above right) should always contain a light.

ABOVE Twin pedestal lavatories in a bathroom (not visible here) might be considered somewhat *de trop* and set the imagination reeling—but what luxury indeed to have the kind of accessory behind the glass observation wall: a narrow 40-foot (12-meter) pool for exercise swimming. The office is on the ground floor beneath it. Not for the fainthearted to attempt at home; the pool's construction was made possible by the fact that the structure is naturally strong enough to support the weight. Installation involved hoisting a single-piece fiberglass pool shell, like a giant bathtub, onto the roof.

ABOVE RIGHT Midnight-blue volcanic lava is used as a combined basin and shelf in this teak-paneled bathroom (*see also* left). This blue was the only concession to color in the apartment. The materials used are not commonplace, but utterly luxurious and their pitted surfaces are full of character. Curved old-fashioned faucets on washbasins and bathtubs can look quite sculptural.

BATHROOMS

A friend of mine, the slightly eccentric and utterly chic Clair Watson—ex-fashion director, now conceptual artist, an Englishwoman in New York—offers the most enjoyable bathing experience imaginable at her home in the Hamptons. There is no bathroom involved, just an outdoor shower, a hose and rose affair attached to a wall on the back of the house, with nothing but the elements as witness. After a long walk on the beach, it is heavenly. And there we have it, the bathing experience, the simplest and most gratifying function performed inside—or outside—the home.

In 1933, the Japanese writer Junichiro Tanizaki wrote a thought-provoking essay entitled In *Praise of Shadows*, in which he attempted to define Japaneseness in the face of modernity. It is an amusing, flowing commentary on beauty, architecture, drama, food, and many other aspects of the clash of traditions. Tanizaki describes an aesthetic of shadows which, according to him, embodies pure Japanese culture. Everything essential takes place in the corners, silences, and interstices of life. He describes an experience in traditional Kyoto where going to the bathroom (and I don't mean to take a bath) becomes a spiritual epiphany: the character walks from the main house across a bridge to a cabinet without a roof, as if going to bathe in a Japanese hot spring, a tradition that elevates everyday need to hedonistic ritual. The description of the sound of rainwater and the rustling of leaves reminds me of the simplicity of Ms. Watson's bathing facility. In a home, we cannot recreate the sensations of alfresco bathing—the air against the skin, the vistas—and there is the added issue of that man-made phenomenon, decency. We can, however, keep the bathroom simple, tranquil, and relatively unadorned.

Bathing may be a simple function, but the bathroom has become an uneasy mix of clashing traditions, of old-world washing facility and modern design. Designers frequently have an aesthetic in mind when designing a bathroom that I find too clinical, and it often fails the acid test. There are some good-looking washrooms in restaurants and hotels these days which, I am sorry to say, do not work. I constantly witness what I call the bathroom shuffle: woman leaves stall, approaches basin, washes hands; puts handbag between legs while shuffling to air dryers on opposite wall; re-approaches basin to tend to

makeup; leans toward mirror above basin. Result: a line of water from basin edge across woman's skirt; she shuffles back to air dryer to dry skirt, bag at this stage clasped between upper arm and rib cage and also wet by now. An extreme example perhaps, but it illustrates how dysfunctional a bathroom can become. A mirror above a basin is a good idea, but there should also be another nearby for close scrutiny or for contact-lens wearers, who are always losing lenses down drain holes. Some bathrooms are dual purpose (*see* page 152), which calls for ingenuity, especially on the storage front. A "his and hers" bathroom might require two vanity units to accommodate the daily routines of two very different

ABOVE Plain biscuit-colored mosaic tiles bordered in black are relatively easy to keep clean and add depth and texture to the room. Highly colored and decorative mosaics are not usually a good idea for townhouses and apartments because they tend to tire. This bathroom has a neoclassical feel because of the materials used, although the lines are modern.

LEFT The corridor between Jean-Dominique Bonhotal's living room and bedroom is home to a magnificent wash basin. Facing it, a door opens up to reveal the rest of the bathroom. The combination of materials used is as well thought-out as throughout the rest of the apartment.

LEFT AND BELOW Bathing is an ancient pastime, for cleansing and relaxation. It was in Rome, in the great *thermae*, that the bath received its most complete architectural form. There were bathrooms in early Egyptian palaces, but the remains are too fragmentary for analysis. The Aegean civilization provides the earliest well-preserved examples of bathrooms, remarkable for their structure and advanced systems of water supply and drainage. Bathing has never been out of fashion; it is not so widely known, but the Romans gave up their bathing activities only because of the destruction of their great aqueducts. A single piece of furniture or object can add personality to a bathroom (left)—here an African chair, both attractive and useful. It is no longer considered unattractive for the bones of bathroom accouterments to be visible: we are long over the boxed-in bathtub and, as with furniture legs, would rather see the structure. There is something very innocent and demure about this single exposed washbasin (below). Metals (non-corrosive ones such as stainless steel or nickel- or chrome-plated varieties) and glass are a fine combination in rooms of function.

people. Whatever the situation, the approach should be as simple and as pared down as possible.

My grandmother used to quote a saying that before you leave home you should look in the mirror, turn away, and then look again. The first thing you see on second glance should be removed, since it will be the least necessary accessory. The same applies to bathrooms. Modern life does not necessarily need modern design, just common sense. The bathing experience should take place in the spiritual corners and silences of a home. A bathroom is one room that can be reduced to very little: gimmicks and gadgetry have no place in the classic bathroom.

STUDIES

A century ago, the study was the most forbidding room in the home—for women at least. For the man of the house, it was like a potting shed, an escape from the reality of family life: returning from work or his club, he would go to his study to work more, smoke cigars, read, write, or just think. A gentlewoman would not have had the privilege of her own study, a fact ardently lamented. "A woman must have money and a room of her own if she is to write fiction," wrote Virginia Woolf in her 1928 essay entitled *A Room of One's Own*. But

LEFT Collett and Zarzycki turned a connecting room between bedrooms into a study for their client, overlooking the gardens. The Chinese lamps add majesty to the relatively diminutive room. Even in a large house, many cannot afford the luxury of a full-size office. A desk for writing letters is always lovely in or near a bedroom. The carpet was designed by Christopher Farr.

BELOW I was told years ago that the most useful tool for a writer is a wastepaper basket, something I have not forgotten. I was also told that there is no such thing as "work to do": it is either done or about to be done. Jackie Villevoye, a busy mother of five as well as a successful interior designer, has been taught the same lesson, it seems. This storage system can be emulated using many materials, from cardboard to metal. Note the unusual square recessed spotlights.

BELOW In a Manhattan scheme by Thad Hayes, cantilevered rosewood shelves, with delightful butterfly joints visible, span the breadth of a wall. "The built-in furniture bridges the architecture and the freestanding pieces," he says. "I wanted to develop a modern, seamless interior, where they [the clients] could move easily between uncluttered rooms."

women could not expect privacy at all—moreover, it was considered dangerous for a woman to be alone with her thoughts. And heaven forbid if a member of the gentle sex aspired to live alone, a longing portrayed beautifully in Edith Wharton's *The House of Mirth* (published in 1905): "She noticed the letters and notes heaped upon the table among his gloves and sticks, then she found herself in a small library, dark but cheerful, with its walls of books, a pleasantly faded Turkey rug, a littered desk, and as he had foretold, a tea-tray on a low

table near the window. A breeze had sprung up, swaying inward the muslin curtains and bringing a fresh scent of mignonette and petunias from the flower box on the balcony. Lily sank into one of the shabby leather chairs. 'How delicious to have a place like this all to one's self! What a miserable thing it is to be a woman.'"

Thank goodness for women's emancipation. There must have been an awful lot of women hungry for that shabby leather chair and a wall lined with books, a place to call their own. Curiously, the

LEFT A room of one's own: Holly Hunt has a hectic life traveling between offices in Chicago and New York. "Find something you love to do," she says, "because you spend a long time doing it." Her own bedroom is deeply serene, sporting an antique desk, one of the few vestiges from her past, upon which sit a few carefully chosen objects. Like Coco Chanel, one of her muses, Hunt does nothing by accident.

ABOVE Another home office for a busy creative soul, this time that of fashion and celebrity portrait photographer Matthew Rolston, in the house he shares with Ted Russell. As in the rest of the house, wide windows maximize daylight and neutral hues create a quiet refuge from glamour and bright lights.

LEFT Jean-Dominique Bonhotal's oak-shelved study is light, moody, and almost spiritual. The mahogany desk and table are his own designs, and the red "Vivette" armchair is by Luca Meda for Molteni. A fireplace and deep-pile rug make the room cozy in winter; doors to the terrace refresh the mood in summer.

turn-of-the-twentieth-century Parisienne, while slightly freer, had a different problem, evident from paintings of the era. Her subordination was accomplished by treating women as part of the décor. Bourgeois wives were not to select fabrics according to fashion, but to pick those that suited their hair color and skin tone: blondes were said to be best offset by sea green, sky blue, or cherry red, while brunettes were flattered by backgrounds of deep blue, olive, or gold. The theory was adopted in 1924 by Max Factor, the inventor of commercial makeup, who made up his models in appropriately colored rooms. Still painted blue (blonde), pink (brunette), and green (redhead), these rooms can be seen at the original Max Factor offices in Los Angeles, now a museum of makeup.

Today, if you have the luxury of a study—and it is a luxury, fulfilling a need for order as well as refuge—be aware that it will reveal your true self more than any other room. As writer Marcelle Tinayre puts it, "When an unknown visitor awaits us... he first meets our objects, the witnesses and confidants of our lives."

A study does not always need to be neat, but it must be organized, with everything to hand. There are many and various ways of doing this, some quite extreme. Designer Ashley Hicks, son of the late great designer David Hicks, organizes his books by color, which seems a little pretentious until he points out that he has a good visual memory and a hopeless memory otherwise, and can readily extract from his brain the color of the book he is seeking rather than whether he placed a book

about design history, for example, along with tomes on art, or those on history.

Nowadays many people work from home; the study is where most of their time is spent, and so tends less to be a room for relaxation and more a venue for clarity of mind. I think computers should be kept on view, ready for action, as long as they are as slinky as possible and their accouterments—the cables and wires that have unfortunately become part of our interior landscape—concealed. Nowadays time means money more than ever before, and there is no point in wasting precious minutes shifting equipment.

REPOSE

People, like furniture, can be vertically or horizontally inclined. I tend to be the former, since many of my daily activities require walking around the home. I sometimes have in mind that image from Fritz Lang's *Metropolis* of a dynamic and ever-moving city. In the movie, Lang (a former architect) imagined an orderly city-state of monumental structures, micromanaged by an authoritarian technocrat. Despite criticisms, the film is one of the most expressive testimonies of its time, revealing conflicts, hopes, fears, and its characters' enthusiasm for technology and for the American way—and using powerfully evocative architectural metaphors. In many ways the home resembles such a city in miniature, although without the slaves laboring underground at gigantic machines.

If I am not walking around my apartment, which Americans would call a "classic six" since there are six principal rooms (we live in the first "mansion block" to be built in mid-nineteenth-century London—the first experiment in lateral living on a reasonable scale), I tend to sit at a desk or at a table to dine, and rarely recline unless I am in bed. Although I admire the form of the Le Corbusier chaise, for example, it does not hold a special place in my heart for the simple reason that the amount of space it requires does not equate with the amount of time I might lounge on it. My husband, on the other hand, is a horizontal being when he is not working, and enjoys lounging in chairs and on sofas. The children seem to enjoy his attention in this state of repose and mine while I am active.

Dining rooms and studies are my passions, but for most people the living room is the nest. In the past, many houses had three "living" rooms: a morning room, a parlor, and a drawing room or salon, the first two less formal than the last. The formal living room had been the medieval great chamber, high-ceilinged and hung with rich tapestries, a public room used for formal gatherings and feasts. The informal living room began life as a "withdrawing room," often a private space adjoining a bedroom. Over time, expensive furnishings, elaborate tables, collections of artifacts, and fabric hangings were introduced. In grand houses, the great chamber evolved into a gallery, and the informal living room into a room for cards and other pleasure pursuits. The parlor existed in modest homes and was used only on special occasions. People lived this way throughout the Victorian and Edwardian periods, and some still prefer to maintain two living rooms, one a "den" or "media room," the other more formal. Gradually, however, the rooms became more multipurpose, and most of us today have just one, best termed a "living room."

Repose rooms generally require ambient rather than task lighting, and relatively soothing color palettes (*see* pages 82–85). Since movement is not a priority, there is less need for space, and furniture can be drawn together in user-friendly islands.

In a repose area in a home "gymnasium" in London's Notting Hill, an African bench carved from a single piece of wood by the Senuso people of the Ivory Coast languishes upon an unusual carpet made from recycled paper. The gym equipment is concealed behind a nineteenth-century Egyptian screen, which allows the free flow of air throughout. Outside is a sun deck.

ABOVE A modern living room that encompasses all
aspects of living, dining, and study can retain a level
of salubrity and serenity as well as offering details of
character: the client's collection of Gallé vases rests
on a custom-designed multipurpose table that serves
to anchor the room. "It's the only place where
decorative objects are encouraged to move around,"
says Robert Bray. The layout of the room, reassuringly
symmetrical, encourages a sense of repose. Richard
Giglio's *Word Painting*, from 1997, is the only
permanent element above eye level.

LIVING ROOMS

Living rooms are generally for relaxation and entertainment: they thus have a dual purpose and need to function adequately for both. Comfortable furniture is vitally important, and a room with enough seating for the inhabitants alone will need a supporting cast that can be brought into the frame at a moment's notice. Occasional chairs fulfill this function, although I do not think it elegant to drag furniture in from another room when guests arrive. Chairs placed around the perimeter of the room can be brought into the main seating arrangement if there is enough room, and a chaise longue can be useful since, although intended for one person, it can easily accommodate more.

Upholstered footstools are rarely used for feet any more, but are discreet and good for sitting on as a last resort. Interior designer Jenny Armit has solved the problem of extra seating by designing a large square ottoman that functions as a coffee-table in two quarter sections, which are wooden-topped; the other two sections are upholstered in leather to accommodate books or people. An ottoman, like a coffee-table, acts as a reassuring barrier between people who do not know one another; in cube form, it also straightens the look of a room, lending harmony and balance.

Seating arrangements can form cozy islands, and many designers create two or more such areas in one room, if it is large enough, rather than a single seating plan. This can result in too much distance between people, which is not conducive to conversation. Jean-Dominique Bonhotal's Paris home (see pages 14–15) has two seating areas, but the furniture is on

ABOVE RIGHT An informal living area to one end of a vast "play room," which also contains an antique billiard table, offers quiet respite. The fireplace is not grand but serves its function; the pairs of chairs and footstools suggest leisure. In this room, Stephen Sills wanted to create an atmosphere of shaded light and rich texture.

wheels or castors so the two islands can readily be amalgamated. A good system, if you have space, is to have a pair of sofas back to back (not necessarily hugging each other, and it is better if they are different but with similar proportions), with pairs of chairs opposite each sofa. Not only can the symmetry add to the room's neatness (living rooms tend to be easily disrupted), but the arrangement makes for entertaining social events, since guests can move from one group to another.

ABOVE It might seem odd to have a fireplace as a focal point in a Los Angeles house, but this is on a hilltop plateau way above the city and has its own microclimate. Cacti grow outside, yet throughout the day mist forms around the house—it is really quite refreshing. The floor-level fireplace is needed when the temperature drops, and the combination of richly textured carpets and colder floors suits the peculiar climate. Restfulness is achieved by balancing the varying needs. The painting, Mike Berg's *Untitled Branch with Rose*, somehow magically distills the nectar of the room.

Tucked away in a corner of a Manhattan apartment, a sturdy leather daybed, chair, and lamp await anyone in need of putting their feet up or a good read. A spare bedroom can be adapted for living by day and guests by night. The daybed had its inception in France and was used for sleeping on at night, too; it was popularized in America when apartment living became *de rigueur*. Original delicate French daybeds, of course, will not accommodate a twenty-first-century-sized guest overnight, so be sure to choose a bed of enough breadth and width if the intent is to double up its use.

Just as it is considered wrong to place furniture in front of a window, without a gap, especially if the window is full length or opens, it is also better not to place sofas and armchairs right against a wall: even if it means more space in the center, it will make the room seem less spacious. A sofa or armchair, particularly if plump or wide, needs room to breathe, spatially speaking.

Many living rooms have a fireplace which is ideal as a focal point. In a scheme by Jonathan Reed in London, the living room is centered around a look-through fireplace, a perfect way to compartmentalize a room that serves two functions, and provide relatively cosy comfort in a large space. One seating arrangement, including an Eames chair, faces the fireplace on one side of the fireplace wall; on the other side is a more comfortable sofa, also facing the fireplace. Freestanding chimney frames are not new: they were all the rage in the 1960s and '70s, when designer Max Clendinning built them from scratch.

A good way to create a large room that works well for our modern era is to convert two backing fireplaces into one by removing the wall between the rooms. The result is open-plan and comfortable, although advice may be needed on air circulation for the fire. In all cases, fireplaces should be generous and not look bleak when the fire is unlit.

Living rooms need side tables, since in repose, unless we are sleeping, we generally have something at hand—a book,

ABOVE Some of the most engaging rooms, whether for repose or activity, follow the simplest possible forms of organization. Andrzej Zarzycki's principal living room is a paean to the traditional seating arrangement, yet its effect is wholly modern: the epitome of new classic. Another interesting point about this room is that not one piece of furniture is recognizable—Collett-Zarzycki almost always custom-design furniture for their schemes. The copper fire surround is highly unusual; the intention was for it to develop a patina over time.

ABOVE A multipurpose room needs an anchor, here the sofa. The symmetry on the back wall is only slightly offset by the differences in the lamp bases and ethnic objects, which at least appear related. In a room where many objects live together, it is important to have a linking theme, or a thread, to avoid looking too "eclectic," heaven forbid. "Eclectic" groupings should be objects from disparate origins that sit well together. Here, Collett used the building's traditional baseboards, architraves, panelled doors, and molding—softened to make it more tactile. Walls are also textured.

newspaper, or drink. They may also need cabinets and console tables for the tools of living. Cabinets and bureaus can bring a majestic feel to a living room through their size and, if lovingly crafted, elegance. A well-chosen chest is also a good addition, again because of its craftsmanship.

Whether you sit for hours in repose or play a card game or two, the living room, like the dining room, should not be valued for what it contains so much as for the feelings of contentment it evokes.

LEFT A "D'Urso" table by Knoll and a set of six chairs by the Viennese Josef Hoffman make up the dining "room" of the Neutra house, making a statement of character and originality. The chairs—designed in 1904 for the Purkersdorf Sanatorium, where dozens of them were lined up along both sides of a long narrow table—make good side chairs, too, so they are perfect for use in a space where flexibility is crucial. On the table is a pair of silver vases decorated with a thumbprint dent, by Elsa Peretti for Tiffany. The painting is by James Nares.

RIGHT, ABOVE The table top is the final grooming of a dining room, a hairstyle that can be dressed to suit any occasion. Tablecloths are unnecessary when a table possesses its own beauty; while there is nothing lovelier than crisp white linen cloths under an entertainment tent in summer or when you are dining *al fresco*, a table indoors should never be so ugly that it has to be hidden.

RIGHT This dining room is flexible and austere enough to be used as a conference room by day (although conference chairs should have arms). By night it takes on another guise. A dining chair must be able to fit underneath the table to at least halfway. Pedestal tables work best for dining, because tables with legs always require a degree of negotiation, unless the table is square or circular and has legs very clearly visible at its edge. The design and materials used dictate the structural support required; long rectangular or banquet tables today have the advantage of new structural technology over those of yesteryear.

DINING ROOMS

"All the arts are chic... don't ask me why," observed French novelist Etincelle in *Carnet d'un mondain* in 1882; the art of dining well and with ease is no exception. It is crucial to be able to relax in the dining room, since guests who feel uncomfortable can hardly walk out midway without causing a kerfuffle. A dining room is like a boat out of dock: you have to deal with all eventualities before reaching dry land.

The idea of a separate room for eating became the norm in middle- and upper-class European homes in the eighteenth century. Up to this point, the nobility ate at long tables in spacious halls or at smaller tables in a dining area of a living room. The increasing informality of late-eighteenth-century society saw the dining room develop in its own right, as an adjunct and counterbalance to the drawing room.

A dining room has potential for great character since it has two faces: by day and by night. Good lighting is invaluable, whether ambient lighting, chandeliers, or candles are used: be sure to try it out at various times of day. The room can become

very theatrical once dusk falls, and a good host should make sure of the delights not only of the food and wine served, but also of the interior. Subtle color palettes are most conducive to good appetite, although grander gestures can also work. Bear in mind that purples and blues retain their depth by candlelight, whereas reds disappear in dim lighting (*see* page 75).

A perky catalog published last century by the French department store Galeries Lafayette questioned attitudes toward design: "The same bibelots on the same tables? The same curtains?... You stop at nothing to be original in your toilette and you are right to do so; your hats are yours and yours alone.... You can be sure the décor you live in is just as important." A catalog after my own heart. How dull it would be to swan from dinner to dinner and house to house, only to experience similar décors. The dining room is surely a room for statement and originality.

The shape and size of the room generally dictate the shape and size of the table. Rectangular rooms that are not too long look best with square or rectangular tables, although they should not have the same proportions as the room; square rooms look best with tables that are circular, oval,

ABOVE The polished mahogany French dining table dates from the end of the Louis Philippe period, the chairs with cloverleaf cutout motif to the reign of his predecessor, Charles X. Their curved form makes a good alternative to the more usual (in traditional homes, at least) balloon-backed version. Sills and Huniford did not consciously select nineteenth-century furniture for this house of the same period: the pieces they found simply fitted in with the whole scheme. A dining room does not have to be "in period" to be a classic. With the right intuition, old can mix with new and vice versa.

BELOW A table top usually needs protection: place mats can suffice. A well-dressed table should sport underplates, too. For a while the world was bereft of good flatware design and had to rely on old-fashioned shell-motif or beaded silver, or stylish but predictable Danish stainless flatware. Now designers are again creating interesting pieces from classic materials such as silver and ebony, and less classic but equally interesting ones such as bronze and resin.

ABOVE Ten can sit quite comfortably in the small dining room of this Los Angeles cottage. The room was never intended to be a formal dining room, but Armit's ingenuity—hanging a chandelier and making best use of the floor space by placing nothing in the room but table and chairs—has elevated its relaxed nature while providing comfort for dining. The table and bowl are new, and their resin base is warm to the touch, as is the wood of the dining chairs. The flooring is original: removed, restored, replaced, stained, and polished. The sheer black curtains bring added glamour.

or square. Long rooms can support only long tables, which should not be too wide, since conversation will be stilted if diners can talk only to the person on their right or left. Circular tables are best if they seat eight to twelve people. The diameter may inhibit conversation, but the curvature allows people to talk to those one place beyond their neighbors. To my mind, the circular table wins hands down in terms of elegance of form and usefulness.

Dining tables should be central or almost central to a room—symmetry is always attractive—and the accompanying chairs must have either no arms or arms that fit

beneath the table top. There must be space for people to walk behind the chairs when they are pulled out. Sideboards are useful, not only to contain flatware and napkins, but also as another platform on which to place things. Granite-topped sideboards can be beautiful, stylish, and functional.

Table decoration should be minimal, and either low or streamlined: too many tables are heavily adorned with objects that add nothing. Fabric may contribute to theatricality, but excessive drapery can be claustrophobic and fussy. Glass of any kind, however, adds to the splendor, and the light playing through it can be hypnotic.

Sally Sirkin Lewis's bedroom reveals updated Hollywood-style 1920s chic and comfort. The feminine room is largely unadorned: walls and ceiling lack embellishment, although the walls are fabric-covered in subtle beige. The chair is one of Lewis's own designs: inspired by period and Art Deco lines, but reinterpreting them through scale, her chairs feature "Old World" wood-carving techniques and wood veneers such as light-colored French ash and Macassar ebony. Mirrored furniture also evokes Art Deco.

BEDROOMS

ABOVE This guest room's natural palette brings us down to earth. Too much brown can feel restricting, yet all cultures treasure the beauty of wood, and there are many ways to enjoy natural colors without oppressive dark browns. Ceramics, marble, stone, and plaster also bring natural tones. Here, the touch of glass and silver smartens the earthiness, as does the four-poster bed by Christian Astuguevieille.

The bedroom is the "repose" equivalent of the more "active" study, a private place where we let down our guard and show our true colors. This of course allows a huge amount of scope; as the English actress Mrs. Patrick Campbell (Beatrice Stella Tanner, 1865–1940) put it, "It doesn't matter what you do in the bedroom as long as you don't do it in the street and frighten the horses." A successful bedroom design should truly reflect our most personal tastes and requirements.

According to Samuel Gosling from the University of Texas in Austin, writing in the *Journal of Personality and Social Psychology*, there are such things as bedroom secrets. His

ABOVE The composition of Carlos Aparicio's bedroom was based on the wall design, stuccoed random squares that give the room rhythm (he had the idea when traveling by train). The color palette extends to include the bed. Although chairs and a sofa are squeezed into the room, the effect is not crowded, due to the small scale of the delicate French pieces. The library steps are by Gustave Eiffel.

LEFT Comfort and indulgence mark this room, whose bed niche is reflected in the mirrored closet doors. Having built-in closets saves space for seating and a desk; free-standing closets would also have made the dual-purpose room more bedroomy. The mirrors reflect light and give a feeling of space.

team asked fifteen volunteers to attempt to guess people's characters from observing their bedrooms, with photographs and other clues removed. The assessors did not do well at rating "extroversion, agreeableness or emotional stability," but were remarkably accurate in assessing "conscientiousness and openness," traits that Gosling considered almost impossible to gauge from seeing a person in the flesh. I cannot imagine that many bedrooms would go so far as to contain apparitions like Tracey Emin's bed (the art version, for which collector and advertising mogul Charles Saatchi paid more than $200,000

following its entry for the Turner prize: the disheveled bed certainly showed, as intended, many of Ms. Emin's less savory character traits and a certain degree of extroversion), but even for the rest of us the bedroom evidently speaks volumes.

The venerable Paris-based interior designer Alberto Pinto, one of the most elegant gentlemen I have ever had the pleasure to spend time with, began designing interiors in the 1960s and today creates splendid homes and palaces throughout the world in no particular style but his own—which bends and sways to meet clients' personalities and desires, and cannot be summed up in few words. Although essentially luxurious, his interiors display a restraint that makes you want more, and more. His own recent apartment, overlooking the River Seine, was lavishly decorated, with Ionic columns flanking a *grand salon* entrance with a full-height wrought-iron Directoire door. Seeking to re-create the "muffled comfort of a grand hotel suite," his bedroom was immense, large enough to include a drawing room and study area. At one end, over an American nineteenth-century mahogany sofa upholstered in green velvet, hung a tondo from the *fin de siècle*. The French Empire mahogany bed was surrounded by *capitonné* armchairs ready for friends to slump into (I am not sure if Pinto likes to sit and chat from his bed, but the evidence suggests he does).

In complete contrast, the traditional Japanese bedroom is empty of almost all furniture. Futons and bedding are folded away each day and stored in built-in closets, or hung out to air, giving the *tatami* matting a chance to air, too. In many cases, the room is used as living quarters by day, but even so, furnishing and decoration are minimal—perhaps a low table, cushions, and a small mirror (with a silk cover when not in use, to avoid unwanted glare), all easily pushed to one side to make way for futons. There may be a *tokonoma* or alcove holding a vase with an ikebana arrangement of a few sprigs, above it a scroll of calligraphy or ink painting. Walls are natural wood, off-white wallpaper, or painted cream or muted pale green (often coarsely textured), while windows and doors also make use of natural wood and shoji paper screens that allow in the softest of ambient light. Despite its openness to multiple functions, a room such as this is the epitome of serenity: to step into it is to be instantly soothed. Few of us may choose

ABOVE Somewhat out of character, architect Michael Wolfson chose black-and-white eighteenth-century-designed *toile de Jouy* fabric panels to line the walls of his guest bedroom, a remarkable but classic and effective room. The bleached-oak headboard with inset padded bolster in amoeboid form and the "Zig-zag" cabinet in bleached oak and dark-stained wenge are from Wolfson's custom furniture line. A 1980s vase by Ettore Sottsass and a collection of 1950s Polish Cmielow handpainted porcelain animals add further decoration.

ABOVE A difficult-shaped bedroom can pose problems: you may find, as here, that there is only one place for the bed. The decoration and embellishment of the apartment has been left intact: it adds to its Parisian charm and balances the wrought-iron railings outside the window. To update the scene, Nye Basham has made a bold statement with his rather masculine gray-and-white bed and chic gray silk curtains. Smaller classical French furniture would have been less dynamic. This is a good example of large furniture making a room seem more generous.

to live entirely Japanese-style, but elements of the approach can be incorporated to great effect without seeming out of place.

Whatever their style, multipurpose bedrooms are becoming popular, and I think it is a good idea in this hectic world to live sometimes as if in a hotel suite, with all life's necessities close at hand. Jonathan Reed created a version of this in the bedroom portion of an apartment in London's Cadogan Gardens (*see* page 174), where two busy people can function and relax in a serene atmosphere in some ways reminiscent of a Japanese room, achieved by using pale and muted beige tones. There is a living room for formal entertainment.

Bedrooms may be used primarily for repose, but they nonetheless require fluency of movement when necessary. The bed is always the main feature, bedside tables the supporting cast—everything else is incidental. The symmetry of a bed cues symmetry at either side, so drawers integral to the bed frame are welcome. Both sparsely and densely furnished bedrooms can be elegant, as long as ease of movement is not sacrificed in the latter.

Elegant bedrooms have existed since ancient times. While the ancestors of the British were sleeping on piles of skins and moss not far removed from a hedgehog's heap of leaves, others lived in legendary splendor. In the Old Testament, kings lounged on "beds... of gold and silver upon a pavement of... marble." The bronze beds of Assyrian potentates were encrusted with precious stones. For the Greeks and Romans, the bed was a focus of social life; the Greek *kline* (which gives us the word "recline"), with its low headrest, was a slim, elegant affair that was used for eating.

The bed as we know it began its ascendancy in the thirteenth century, when it also acquired a canopy. Bed curtains kept out persistent drafts and cold, but the

primary role of the canopy or tester was to symbolize rank and power; it was originally the prerogative of kings and statesmen.

Today, with heating in almost all homes, curtained beds are no longer necessary. In hot climates we are more likely to drape a four-poster with netting to keep out animal life. I do not have a penchant for heavily draped canopied beds, since they tend to block the sight-line. As I like to walk up to windows, I like to see where a window is. Also, the dust collected by a canopied bed

is surely not good for us. This was noted by Carl Larsson, popularizer of those white, bright bedrooms with simple cotton curtains that epitomized Swedish design of the early twentieth century, replacing the cosily boxed-in beds that had persisted through chill Scandinavian winters.

I do, however, enjoy the elegant forms of some four-poster beds (*see* page 116), which can be sculptural and bring another dimension to a taller bedroom where the rest of the furniture is considerably lower.

ABOVE Prevailing symmetry and a sense of precision can extend to the bedroom. A headboard is useful visually because it frames the head of the bed, and practically because it is needed for sitting up to read in bed and, last but not least, prevents wall damage behind the bed. Rather like doors and chair backs, the height of the head of a bed can express grandeur if it is tall, and subtlety if it is less tall, but it should always be firm to lean against. Quality sheets and coverlets are a must for a stylish bed. The bedside tables are by Bray-Schaible.

Mahogany is a delicious wood for a period bed—for Directoire or French Empire as preferred by Alberto Pinto, for example—but newer four-posters look crisper in woods such as teak, light oak, or wenge.

Bedrooms can be disappointing, along with bathrooms, in even the most "designed" homes, since generally less attention is given to areas where guests spend less time. This is a terrible mistake: the most successful decorative schemes are consistent, so treat bedrooms with as much

concern as the living room, taking into account especially issues such as lighting and color (*see* pages 60–67 and 74–85).

Accommodating a couple in one bedroom is a challenge. In grander homes of the past, bedrooms were personal chambers: husband and wife slept apart. While this may not be viable today, it has advantages, as two personalities rarely coincide on such a fundamental level. A well-designed bedroom, however, can make a harmonious couple even happier.

INDOOR OUTDOOR

"There's no music like a little river's. It plays the same tune (and that's the favorite) over and over again, and yet does not weary of it like men fiddlers. It takes the mind out of doors; and though we should be grateful for good houses, there is, after all, no house like God's out-of-doors," wrote Robert Louis Stevenson in 1885. Not all of us are blessed with a yard, let alone a river, but today there is no greater status symbol and no better psychological comfort than an outdoor space of some sort, whether a roof terrace, interior garden, or full-blown acreage. And what better way to have an audible reminder of the great outdoors than a simple fountain, indoors or out?

In many homes, inside and outside are interwoven. Interiors are expanded outward with exterior seating, outdoors brought in by using the verdure of nature in a solarium, or visually by maximizing windows and views. Modernist architecture followed this philosophy (see pages 32–33),

ABOVE The indoor orangery at the end of the enfilade of rooms stretching from front to back of Holly Hunt's home has existed since the previous tenant's time: it seduced Hunt with its light and freshness. The parquet floor vanishes at this point, and the orangery is given a more outdoor feel by square-tiled flooring. White slipcovers, often used on outdoor seating or inside in summer months, cover the armchairs. How heavenly to feel as if you are in a country solarium when you are actually in a city.

ABOVE It takes imagination to create such a long room: I cannot remember seeing a more chic and enticing dining room, "decorated" chairs standing with military order en route to the garden. Its trees and shrubbery precision-cut, the garden is as wide as the house and entirely symmetrical; the section beyond the dining room to one side of this Dutch house has been designed to continue the sight-line from the house. Outdoor lighting and clever interior lighting mean that a balance can be found to produce more, or less, dramatic moods at night.

and it is said that designer Eileen Gray plotted the sun's direction for a year before building her house at Roquebrune-Cap-Martin in France, to be sure that inside and outside worked as one.

Gardens follow similar design principles to interiors. Symmetry is key in the ornamental, rigidly geometric "Italian style" popular in England until the eighteenth century. French gardens, too, particularly from the reign of the Sun King, tend to be formal and manicured. At Saint

Germain-en-Laye, west of Paris, the chateau grounds exemplify the ordered creations of royal gardener Le Nôtre around 1700. But beyond the exquisite avenues of walkways and cropped trees is also an "English garden," where tumbling plants reign.

English gardens are indeed less formal, whether they are fluid "cottage" gardens or the landscaped grounds of grand houses. Following Alexander Pope's appeal for the "friendly simplicity of untouched nature," the likes of William Kent (1685–1748) designed gardens with landscape painting in mind, while the rambling landscapes of Lancelot "Capability" Brown (1716–83) planned for informality. Brown dominated British landscape gardening for thirty-five years, visualizing the "capabilities of a property's improvement" and convinced that nature was more beautiful than anything man-made. His work included schemes at Blenheim and Chatsworth.

Contrived versions of nature are even more evident in Japanese gardens. From stunted bonsai, through the intricate lawns and ponds of Katsura Imperial Villa in Kyoto, to the abstraction of a Zen garden, the intention is to create artificially something that symbolizes the natural world. A Zen garden is philosophically a landscape where the viewer can experience profound stillness and calm: islands floating in a sea of sand, mountains rising above mist. A "garden of nothingness," with no plants save moss, it developed around the fifteenth century, influenced by ink painting. At Ryoan-ji, a Zen temple in Kyoto, a plot 35 feet by 100 (10 meters by 30) has gravel raked into lines around fifteen rocks in groups of five, three, and two. The composition generates grace and serenity, inspiring meditation.

Few gardens are achieved without some contrivance. Mathematically, the "golden ratio" is a proportion (1.618, or

ABOVE The ultimate in outdoor living. In Beverly Hills, part of the house has been extended to form a garden "room" that includes a fireplace. The effect is of a room existing outdoors, although only one wall borders the space. Enclosed and private, part garden, part sculpture gallery, it includes a brushed aluminum standing sculpture by Isamu Noguchi and a John Duss patinated steel piece above the mantel.

approximately 8:5) that occurs throughout nature and history, and which we instinctively find beautiful. So, to maximize the aesthetic appeal of a rectangular flower-bed, for instance, the ratio of the long side to the short side should be 1.618.

Garden design follows principles similar to those for interiors. Like a living room, a garden reflects its owner's nature, their generosity or mathematical mind; it should not appear too newly planted. A lawn, like a sofa, is an enticement to linger at leisure.

ABOVE Neutra, architect of this home, aimed to integrate the house into the landscape. A commentary by Cranston Jones read: "Continuity between interior and exterior is maintained through carrying the same terrazzo flooring without change from living area to patio, so that the house, as such, becomes merely controlled environment caught behind glass between floor and roof."

DIRECTORY

INTERIOR DESIGNERS AND ARCHITECTS

Carlos Aparicio Associates
30 East 67th Street
New York
NY 10021
Tel: (212) 794-3642
Fax: (212) 794-5201

Jenny Armit Design and Decorative
   Art Inc.
3425 La Sombra Drive
Los Angeles
CA 90068
Tel: (323) 851-5568
Fax: (323) 851-5569
www.jennyarmit.com

Nye Basham
21 rue d'Argenteuil
75001 Paris
France
Tel: 01 42 60 01 07

Jean-Dominique Bonhotal
12 rue Alfred de Vigny
75008 Paris
France
Tel: 01 56 79 10 80
Fax: 01 56 79 10 89

Booth Hansen Associates/
   Laurence Booth
555 South Dearborn Street
Chicago
IL 60605
Tel: (312) 427-0300

Bray-Schaible Design Inc.
80 West 40th Street
New York
NY 10018
Tel: (212) 354-7525
Fax: (212) 921-5982

Martin Brudnizki Design Studio
Unit 2L, Chelsea Reach
79–89 Lots Road
London SW10 0RN
England
Tel: 020 7376 7555
Fax: 020 7376 7444
www.mbds.net

Collett-Zarzycki
Fernhead Studios
2b Fernhead Road
London W9
England
Tel: 020 8969 6967

Thad Hayes Design, Inc.
90 West Broadway
New York
NY 10007
Tel: (212) 571-1234

Terry Hunziker Incorporated
208 Third Avenue South
Seattle
WA 98104
Tel: (206) 467-1144
Fax: (206) 467-7061

David Kleinberg Design Associates
330 East 59th Street
New York
NY 10022
Tel: (212) 754-9500

Christian Liaigre
61 rue Varenne
75007 Paris
France
Tel: 01 47 53 78 76
and
42 rue du Bac
75007 Paris
France
Tel: 01 53 63 33 66

Frédéric Méchiche
4 rue Thorigny
Paris 75003
France
Tel: 01 42 78 78 28

Mlinaric, Henry and Zervudachi Limited
38 Bourne Street
London SW1W 8JA
England
Tel: 020 7730 9072
Fax: 020 7823 4756

Andrée Putman sarl
83 avenue Denfert-Rochereau
75014 Paris
France
Tel: 01 55 42 88 55

Jonathan Reed/Reed Design
151a Sydney Street
London SW3 6NT
England
Tel: 020 7565 0066

Daniel Romualdez Architects
119 West 23rd Street, Suite 710
New York
NY 10011
Tel: (212) 989-8429
Fax: (212) 989-8986

Ted Russell
Tel: (310) 275-1609
Fax: (310) 271-4478

John Saladino/Saladino Group
200 Lexington Avenue
New York
NY 10016
Tel: (212) 684-6805

Sally Sirkin Lewis
J. Robert Scott
8737 Melrose Avenue
Los Angeles
CA 90069
Tel: (310) 659-4910

Shelton, Mindel & Associates
216 West 18th Street
New York
NY 10011
Tel: (212) 243-3939

Sills Huniford Associates
30 East 67th Street
New York
NY 10021
Tel: (212) 988-1636

Jackie Villevoye Interior Architect
(Breda, Netherlands)
Fax: 0765 60 11 00

Michael Wolfson Architect
(London, England)
Tel: 020 7630 9377

FURNITURE STORES AND SHOWROOMS

ABC Carpet & Home
881 and 888 Broadway
New York
NY 10003
Tel: (212) 473-3000
www.abchome.com
Eight-floor department store of home furnishings
including vintage furniture

L'Art de Vivre
978 Lexington Avenue
New York
NY 10021
Tel: (212) 734-3510
Eclectic furniture gallery

Breukelen
68 Gansevoort Street
New York
NY 10014
Tel: (212) 645-2216
Sensuous contemporary furniture and accessories
from young European designers

Cappellini Modern Age
102 Wooster Street
New York
NY 10002
Tel: (212) 966-0669
Cutting-edge designs by today's bright sparks

David Champion
199 Westbourne Grove
London W11 2SB
England
Tel: 020 7727 6016
Ethnic accessories and contemporary European
furniture

David Gill Galleries
60 Fulham Road
London SW3 6HH
England
Tel: 020 7589 5946
and
3 Loughborough Street
London SE11 5RB
England
Tel: 020 7793 1100
Extraordinary contemporary and decorative
furniture and objects

Furniture Co.
818 Greenwich Street
New York
NY 10011
Tel: (212) 352-2010
Select and refined contemporary furniture,
ceramics, and glass

Harrods
The Contemporary Gallery
87–135 Knightsbridge
London SW1X 7XL
England
Tel: 020 7730 1234
www.harrods.com
Re-editions of contemporary classic furniture
and lights

Holly Hunt Ltd.
(in Chicago, New York, Miami,
Washington D.C., and Minneapolis)
Tel: (312) 329-5999
Fax: (312) 258-9513
Showrooms specializing in interior furnishings,
lighting, and textiles

David Linley
60 Pimlico Road
London SW1W 8LP England
Tel: 020 7730 7300
Fax: 020 7730 8869
www.davidlinley.com
Ready- and custom-made quality furniture and
home accessories

Moss
146 Greene Street
New York
NY 10012
Tel: (212) 226-2190
The best of contemporary European and American
furniture and accessories design from the likes of
Edra, Zanotta, and Flos

Pranich & Associates—The Wicker Works
Decoration & Design Building
979 Third Avenue, Suite 1520
New York
NY 10022
Tel: (212) 980-6173
Fax: (212) 980-6174
Contemporary furniture in wicker and hemp

Jérôme Abel Seguin
36 rue Etienne Marcel
75002 Paris
France
Tel: 01 42 21 37 70
Hand-carved wooden artifacts from Indonesia

J. Robert Scott
Decoration & Design Building
979 Third Avenue, Suite 220
New York
NY 10022
Tel: (212) 755-4910
Fax: (212) 755-4957
Designs by Sally Sirkin Lewis

Totem Design Group
71 Franklin Street
New York
NY 10013
Tel: (212) 925-5506
Hot contemporary Swedish designs

Troy
138 Greene Street
New York
NY 10012
Tel: (212) 473-3000
Stylish contemporary furniture, lights, and objects

ANTIQUE AND VINTAGE FURNITURE STORES

Agostino Antiques
808 Broadway
New York
NY 10003
Tel: (212) 533-3355
French and English antiques mixed with
reproductions

Bernd Goeckler Antiques
30 East 10th Street
New York
NY 10003
Tel: (212) 777-8209
European furniture from the eighteenth to
twentieth centuries

Beyul
353 West 12th Street
New York
NY 10014
Tel: (212) 989-2533
Antique Chinese furniture and accessories

Ciancimino Ltd.
99 Pimlico Road
London SW1W 8PH
England
020 7730 9950
Italian and other pieces

Didier Aaron & Cie
32 East 67th Street
New York
NY 10021
Tel: (212) 988-5248
Fine eighteenth-century French furniture

Donzella
17 White Street
New York
NY 10013
Tel: (212) 965-8919
Modern gems by Paul Laszio and Paul Frankl

David Duncan Antiques
227 East 60th Street
New York
NY 10022
Tel: (212) 688-0666
Eighteenth- and nineteenth-century European
furniture

Barry Friedman Ltd
32 East 67th Street
New York
NY 10021
Tel: (212) 794-8950
Bauhaus and Art Nouveau furniture and
accessories

Galerie Chastel Maréchal
5 rue Bonaparte
75006 Paris
France
Tel: 01 40 46 82 61
French 1930s and 1940s furniture and objects

Galerie de Beyrie
393 W. Broadway, 3rd Floor
New York
NY 10012
Tel: (212) 219-9565
Most extensive collection of Jean Royere outside
of Paris

Galerie Vallois
41 rue de Seine
75006 Paris
France
Tel: 01 43 29 50 84
Fine French early to mid-twentieth-century
furniture

Galerie Yves Gastou
12 rue Bonaparte
75006 Paris
France
Tel: 01 53 73 00 10
European 1930s and 1940s furniture and objects

Gueridon
359 Lafayette Street
New York
NY 10003
Tel: (212) 677-7740
Mid-century European furniture and ceramics

Hemisphere
173 Fulham Road
London SW3 6JW
England
Tel: 020 7581 9800
Fine French and Italian mid-twentieth-century
furniture

Karl Kemp & Associates
36 East 10th Street
New York
NY 10003
Tel: (212) 254-1877
French neoclassical and Art Deco furniture

Kentshire Galleries
37 East 12th Street
New York
NY 10003
Tel: (212) 673-6644
English antiques set in beautiful period rooms

Lost City Arts
275 Lafayette Street
New York
NY 10012
Tel: (212) 941-8025
Iconic mid-century pieces by Jacobsen, Aalto,
and Saarinen

H.M. Luther Inc. Antiques
61 East 11th Street
New York
NY 10003
Tel: (212) 505-1485
Antique Swedish furniture

Alan Moss
436 Lafayette Street
New York
NY 10003
Tel: (212) 255-0660
Sexy Art Deco and Art Nouveau furniture
and lighting

1950
440 Lafayette Street
New York
NY 10003
Tel: (212) 995-1950
Twentieth-century plums and the best collection of
George Nakashima in the city

Liz O'Brien
800A Fifth Avenue
New York
NY 10021
Tel: (212) 755-3800
Mid-twentieth-century American furniture

Regeneration
38 Renwick Street
New York
NY 10013
Tel: (212) 741-2102
Twentieth-century gems, including hard-to-find
pieces by Gio Ponti

Reymer-Jourdan Antiques
29 E. 10th Street
New York
NY 10003
Tel: (212) 674-4470
Finest French antiques

Ritter Antik
35 East 10th Street
New York
NY 10003
Tel: (212) 673-2213
Biedermeier Furniture

Niall Smith Antiques
344 Bleecker Street #B
New York
NY 10014
Tel: (212) 941-7354
Urns and everything neoclassical

Themes and Variations
231 Westbourne Grove
London W11 25E
England
Tel: 020 7727 5531
Quality late-twentieth-century furniture and objects

Gordon Watson Ltd.
50 Fulham Road
London SW3 6HH
England
Tel: 020 7589 3108
Fine twentieth-century European furniture and
custom-made objects, such as door handles by
Paul Belvoir

ARCHITECTURAL SALVAGE

Crowther of Syon Lodge
Busch Corner, London Road
Isleworth, Middlesex TW7 5BH
England
Architectural components and statuary

Irreplaceable Artifacts
216 East 125th Street
New York
NY 10035
Tel: (212) 777-2900
www.irreplaceableartifacts.com
Architectural salvage from fine hotels and finer
homes

Lot 76
76 East Houston Street
New York
NY 10012
Tel: (212) 505-8699
From metal advertising signs to porcelain bathtubs
and sinks

Materials Unlimited
2 West Michigan Avenue
Ypsilanti
MI 48197
Tel: (734) 483-6980
New and reclaimed architectural materials,
and antiques

Retrouvius
32 York House
Upper Montagu Street
London W1H 1FR
England
Tel: 020 7724 3387
Architectural salvage company;
by appointment only

Urban Archaeology
143 Franklin Street
New York
NY 10013
Tel: (212) 431-4646
Old jukeboxes, mantels, and other architectural
remnants

FABRICS

Britex Fabrics
146 Geary Street
San Francisco
CA 94108
Tel: (415) 392-2910
Fax: (415) 392-3906
www.britexfabrics.com
An entire world of fabrics under one roof

Chase Erwin
Head Office:
River House
53 Lydden Grove
London SW18 4LW
England
Tel: 020 8875 1222
Fax: 020 8875 1444
Silks, both plain and patterned

Donghia
485 Broadway
New York
NY 10013
Tel: (212) 925-2777
Fax: (212) 925-4819
www.donghia .com
Chic modern fabric and furniture

Edelman Leather
Tel: 1 800 886 TEDY
Leather specialists

Larsen
Decoration & Design Building
979 Third Avenue
New York
NY 10022
Tel: (212) 753-4488
showroom
and
111 Eighth Avenue
Suite 930
New York
NY 10011
Tel: (212) 647-6901
Contemporary classics

Sahco Hesslein—Bergamo Fabrics
Decoration & Design Building
979 Third Avenue, 17th floor
New York
NY 10022
Tel: (212) 888-3333
Fax: (212) 888-3837
www.sahco-hesslein.com
Modern designer fabrics for all uses

Scalamandré
942 Third Avenue
New York
NY 10022
Tel: 1 800 932-4361 (for showroom
locations)
Fine fabrics and trim

FURNITURE MANUFACTURERS

Aero
132 Spring Street
New York
NY 10012
Tel: (212) 966-1500
Thomas O'Brien's 1940s-inspired designs

Albrizzi
139 East 66th Street
New York
NY 10021
Tel: (212) 570-0417
The best Lucite furniture and accessories

Armani Casa
97 Greene Street
New York
NY 10012
Tel: (212) 334-1271
*Fashion house's signature monochromatic,
sleek style*

Baker Furniture
PO Box 1887
Grand Rapids
MI 49501
Tel: 1 800 59BAKER
www.bakerfurniture.com
Collections by Barbara Barry and others

Baker Knapp & Tubbs
200 Lexington Avenue, Suite 300
New York
NY 10016
Tel: (212) 779-8810
Fax: (212) 689-2827
*Formal, transitional, and casual American
furniture; by appointment*

B&B Italia USA Inc.
150 East 58th Street
New York
NY 10155
Tel: 1 800 872-1697
www.bebitalia.it
Quality modern furniture

California Closets
Tel: 1 800 336-9195
www.calclosets.com
Custom-made solutions for storage

Cassina
155 East 56th Street
New York
NY 10022
Tel: (212) 245-2121
*Sleek contemporary Italian furniture by the likes
of Piero Lissoni and Philippe Starck*

DDC
181 Madison Avenue
New York
NY 10016
Tel: (212) 685-0800
Quality modern furniture

Ecart International
11 rue Saint Antoine
75004 Paris, France
Tel: 01 42 78 79 11
Re-editions of twentieth-century classics

Kartell
45 Greene Street
New York
NY 10013
Tel: (212) 966-0669
Plastic pieces by top contemporary designers

The Knoll Group
105 Wooster Street
New York
NY 10012
Tel: (212) 343-4180

Les Migrateurs
188 Duane Street
New York
NY 10013
Tel: (646) 414-8004
Designs by Henri Personnaz

Ligne Roset
250 Park Avenue South
New York
NY 10003
Tel: (212) 685-1099
Sleek contemporary Italian furniture

McGuire Furniture Company
151 Vermont Street
San Francisco
CA 94103
Tel: 1 800 662-4847
*New streamlined furniture, stores throughout
America; write or telephone for brochure*

Herman Miller Inc.
855 East Main Avenue
PO Box 302
Zeeland,
MI 49464
Tel: 1 800 851-1196
www.hermanmiller.com
*Furniture by George Nelson, Vernor Panton,
and others*

Néotu
409 West 44th Street
New York
NY 10036
Tel: (212) 262-9250
www.neotu.com
*Contemporary furniture, soft furnishings and rugs,
in limited editions*

Pucci International
44 West 18th Street, 12th Floor
New York
NY 10011
Tel: (212) 633-0452
*Re-edition Eileen Gray rugs
Items by Olivier Gagnère and Chris Lehreche
and others; by appointment*

Saladino Furniture, Inc.
200 Lexington Avenue, Suite 1600
New York
NY 10016
Tel: (212) 684-3720
Fax: (212) 684-3257
*Fine hand-crafted furniture and upholstered
antiques*

Thonet GmbH
PO Box 1520
3558 Frankenberg
Germany
Tel: 064 51 50 80
Designs by Alvar Aalto and Marcel Breuer

Vitra AG
13 Grosvenor Street
London W1X 9FB
England
*Designs by Charles Eames, Vernor Panton, Jaspar
Morrison, Michele de Lucchi, and Ron Arad*

LIGHTS

Ann-Morris Antiques
239 East 60th Street
New York
NY 10022
Tel: (212) 838-4955
Antique lighting fixtures

Artemide
46 Greene Street
New York
NY 10012
Tel: (212) 925-1588
*Modern lighting by mid-century masters and
contemporary talent*

Patrice Butler
10 Normandy Road
London SW9 6JH
England
Tel/fax: 020 7820 9796
*Custom-made contemporary chandeliers;
by appointment*

Delorenzo
956 Madison Avenue
New York
NY 10021
Tel: (212) 249-7575
Art Deco lighting

Ingo Maurer Making Light
89 Grand Street
New York
NY 10012
Tel: (212) 965-8817
Whimsical modern light fixtures

Nessen
420 Railroad Way
PO Box 187
Mamaroneck
NY 19543
Tel: (914) 698-7799
Manufacturer of sleek designs

Tindle
162 Wandsworth Bridge Road
London SW6 2UQ, England
Tel: 020 7384 1485
Lampshades

Paul Verburg Ltd.
9 Cardinal Mansions
Carlisle Place
London SW1P 1EY, England
e-mail: lights@paulverburg.com
Custom lamps; by appointment

Remains
19 West 28th Street
New York
NY 10001
Tel: (212) 675-8051
Antique lighting fixtures

George N. Antiques
67 East 11th Street
New York
NY 10003
Tel: (212) 505-5599
Antique chandeliers

FLOORING

Amtico
200 Lexington Avenue, Suite 809
New York
NY 10016
Tel: (800) 291-9885
Fax: (212) 545-8382
www.amtico.com
Replicate stone, wood, slate, glass, metals

Ann Sacks Tile & Stone
5 East 16th Street
New York
NY 10003
Tel: (212) 463-8400
And in stores nationwide
Tel: 1 800 278-TILE
www.annsacks.com
Glass, metallic-leafed tiles, ceramic tiles

Artistic Tile
79 Fifth Avenue
New York
NY 10003
Tel: (212) 727-9331
Glass and ceramic tiles

Beauvais Carpets
201 East 57th Street
New York
NY 10022
Tel: (212) 688-2265
Oriental rugs

Beshar's Fine Rugs
1513 First Avenue
New York
NY 10021
Tel: (212) 288-1998
Oriental rugs

Doris Leslie Blau
(New York City)
Tel: (212) 586-5511
*Rare European and Oriental carpets;
by appointment only*

Country Floors
15 East 16th Street
New York
NY 10003
Tel: (212) 627-8300
Ceramic and marble tiles

Einstein-Moomjy
150 East 58th Street
New York
NY 10155
Tel: (212) 758-0900
Wide selection of flokatis and wool rugs

Hastings Bath & Tile
230 Park Avenue South
New York
NY 10003
Tel: (212) 674-9700
Glass tiles and bathroom fittings

Johnson USA Inc.
PO Box 2325
Farmingdale
NJ 07727
Ceramic tiles

Junkers
4920 East Landon Drive
Anaheim
CA 92807
Wooden flooring

Odegard, Inc.
200 Lexington Avenue, Suite 1206
New York
NY 10016
Tel: (212) 545-0069
Hand-loomed Tibetan rugs

Mark Shilen Gallery
109 Greene Street
New York
NY 10012
Tel: (212) 925-3394
Antique rugs from Near and Far East

UK Marble Ltd.
21 Nurcott Road
Hereford HR4 9LW
England
*Marble and granite flooring, paneling, fireplaces
and moldings*

Avena Carpets
Bankfields Mill
Haley Hill
Halifax
West Yorkshire HXE 6ED
England
Tel: 01422 330261
Custom-made carpets

Christine Van Der Hurd
102 Wooster Street
New York
NY 10012
Tel: (212) 343-9070
Colorful, finely made modern carpets

Vermont Structural Slate
P.O. Box 98
Fair Haven
VT 05743
Tel: 1 800 343-1900
www.vermontstructuralslate.com

Waterworks
469 Broome Street
New York
NY 10013
Tel: (212) 966-0605
Fax: (212) 966-6747
And other locations around the northeast
www.waterworks.com
Ceramic bathroom tiles

PAINT

Sherwin-Williams
101 Prospect Ave.
Cleveland,
OH 44115
Tel: (216) 566-2000
www.sherwin-williams.com

Benjamin Moore & Co.
51 Chestnut Ridge Rd.
Montvale
NJ 07645
Tel: (201) 573-9600

TRIM

Chadsworth's Columns
277 North Front St.
Historic Wilmington
NC 28401
Tel: 1 800 COLUMNS

Wendy Cushing Trimmings
G7 Chelsea Harbour Design Centre
London SW10 OXE
England
Tel: 020 7351 5796

Wemyss Houlès
40 Newman Street
London W1P 3EA
England
Tel: 020 7255 3305

LAMINATES

Abet Laminates
60 West Sheffield Avenue
Englewood
NJ 07631
Tel: (201) 541-0701

Du Pont Corian
Barley Mill Plaza
P.O. Box 80012
Wilmington
DE 19880-0012
Tel: 1 800 4-CORIAN

OF INTEREST

The American Society of Interior
   Designers
608 Massachusetts Avenue NE
Washington
D.C. 20002
Tel: (202) 546-3480
www.asid.org

Le Corbusier/Villa Savoye
82 rue de Villers
78300 Poissy
France
Tel: 01 39 65 01 06

Brighton Museum & Art Gallery
4–5 Pavilion Buildings
Church Street
Brighton
East Sussex BN1 1UE
England
Tel: 01273 603005

Brooklyn Museum
200 Eastern Parkway
Brooklyn
NY 11238-6052
Tel: (718) 638-5000

Centraal Museum Utrecht
Agnietenstr. 1
Postbus 2106
3500 GC Utrecht
Netherlands
Tel: 030 36 23 62

Cooper-Hewitt National Design Museum
2 East 91st Street
New York
NY 10036
Tel: (212) 849-8400

Interim Art/Maureen Paley
21 Herald Street
London E2 6JT
England
Tel: 020 7729 4112
Fax: 020 7729 4113
High-end contemporary art

Musée des Arts Décoratifs
107 rue de Rivoli
75001 Paris, France
Tel: 01 44 55 57 50

Musée des Arts Décoratifs de Montreal
2929 rue Jeanne d'Arc
Montreal
Quebec H1W 3W2
Canada
Tel: (514) 259 2575

Museu de les Arts Decoratives
Palau Reial de Pedralbes
Avenida Diagonal, 686
08034 Barcelona
Spain
Tel: 93 280 50 24

Museum of Fine Arts
465 Huntington Avenue
Boston
MA 02115
Tel: (617) 267-9300

Museum of Modern Art
11 West 53rd Street
New York
NY 10019
Tel: (212) 708-9480

Parsons School of Design
66 Fifth Avenue
New York
NY 10011
Tel: (212) 229-8900

Philadelphia Museum of Art
26th Street & Benjamin Franklin Parkway
Philadelphia
PA 19130
Tel: (215) 763-8100

Saarinen/Cranbrook Academy of Art
1221 North Woodward
Bloomfield Hills
MI 48304-2824
Tel: (248) 645-3300

White Cube 2
48 Hoxton Square
London N1 6PB
England
Tel: 020 7930 5373
www.whitecube.com
Contemporary art gallery

WEB-BASED SOURCES

American Decorative Arts
3 Olive Street
Northampton
MA 01060
Tel: 1 800 3MODERN
www.decorativearts.com
Twentieth-century furniture and design resources

PAST PRESENT FUTURE
336 East Franklin Avenue
Minneapolis
MN 55404
Tel: (612) 870-0702
Toll-free: 1 800 801-2523
Fax: (612) 870-9490
www.pastpresentfuture.net
*Classic American furniture and accessories from
the late 1800s to the mid-1970s*

Design Within Reach
Tel: 1 800 944-2233
www.dwr.com
Contemporary furniture

Retromodern.com
805 Peachtree Street
Atlanta
GA 30308
Tel: (404) 724-0093
Toll-free: (877) 724-0093
Fax: (404) 724-0424
www.retromodern.com
*Alessi, Mono, Stelton, and Kartell, as well as other
designer furniture lines*

Unicahome
7540 S. Industrial Road, Suite 501
Las Vegas
NV 89139
Toll-free: 1 888 89-UNICA
www.unicahome.com
Contemporary furniture and accessories

INDEX

ACKNOWLEDGMENTS

The author would like to thank all of the designers and architects who so kindly allowed photography of their work; the home-owners—whose personalities have added greatly to the finished homes—for having the prescience to select the above-mentioned designers and architects; and the other creative spirits who did it all themselves—Keith Day, Peter Sheppard and Maureen Paley.

Thank you, also, to the ebullient Catherine Rubinstein for retaining a sense of humor to the end, to Robin Rout for his unerring eye, and to Jude Garlick for her attention to detail. Furthermore, thank you to Ken Hayden for taking hundreds of superlative shots, and to the uncompromising Jacqui Small.

Last, but by no means least, thank you friends and family.